a quiet place

essays on life and family

PEGGY O'MARA

editor of *Mothering* magazine

The essays in this book orginally appeared in
Mothering magazine between 1992 and 2005.

Published by Mothering Publications
Mothering Magazine, Inc.
P.O. Box 1690
Santa Fe, New Mexico 87504

Edited by Melissa Chianta
Design by Laura Egley Taylor
Front cover photograph by Ana June
Photos opposite page (from top left): 1–3: John Schoenwalter,
4, 5: Jill Feinberg; 6: Tom Hitch; 7–12: Eric Swanson;
13–15: Doug Merriam
Back cover photograph by Doug Merriam

ISBN: 0-914257-19-6

A Quiet Place *is dedicated to my children.*
Thank you Lally, Finnie, Bram, and Nora
for teaching me how to be a mother.

WWW.THRIFTYOWL.COM

contents

introduction

THANK YOU FOR READING MY ESSAYS. I am especially grateful for having been able to write and publish such personal material over the last 30 years. You have been a highly receptive audience and have helped me to grow as a writer and as a parent.

Editing other people's writing has also helped me to grow as a writer. It has taught me to be more dispassionate about my own work. And, publishing an essay on a regular basis has given me the opportunity to hone my writing and improve my craft.

Writing has always been a craft that I have loved. I wrote a short story when I was ten. That year, my greatest pleasure was an unpainted desk that I got for Christmas and filled with special papers, pens, and pencils. I was fascinated with the magnifying-glass paper holder that I also got that Christmas, and I still have one like it on my desk today.

In sixth grade my short essay on the love of books won a writing contest. It wasn't until I was in high school, however, that I recognized my own interest in writing. One of my teachers, Sister Lenora, encouraged my writing and asked me to be an editor for the school newspaper. In my senior year, I had a regular gossip column called "Wandering Wildcat" that appeared on the back page of the newspaper.

Writing for the newspaper and being an editor gave me the confidence to apply to journalism school, and I entered Marquette University in 1965. Within the next two years, however, I lost confidence in myself as a writer. This was the era when women were encouraged to have "something to fall back on," and I simply could not imagine what work I would do with a journalism degree. I had

never known a writer. I decided to become a teacher instead.
I also decided to fall back on teaching because I did poorly
in a creative writing course. The teacher scribbled "boring"
on my papers, and in fact I had few interesting experiences
to write about. Or perhaps I simply didn't know myself well
enough to communicate my experiences to others. Sure that
I wasn't really a writer after all, I transferred into secondary
education with an English major. I was going to be a high
school teacher.

As it turned out, I taught high school for only a few
months. But I continued to keep a journal and found my way
back to writing after my children were born. The process of
birthing my first child in 1974 was an ecstatic experience for
me, and I felt compelled to tell everyone. I wrote an essay
called "In Defense of Motherhood" and submitted it to *New
Age* magazine and to *Redbook*'s new mother contest. Both
publications rejected my piece.

Soon after the article had been returned to me a second
time, I was visiting Albuquerque and saw *Mothering* magazine
in a coffee shop there. It was only the second or third issue of
the magazine. I was awestruck by *Mothering* and wished that
I had started it.

Addie Cranson, then Addie Eavenson, had founded
Mothering in 1976 in southern Colorado. I sent "In Defense of
Motherhood" to Addie, and she immediately accepted it for
Mothering. It was published in issue VII. I sent her a poem,
"There Will Be Time," which she also accepted and published
in issue VIII.

In 1978, just as these pieces were published, I moved to
Albuquerque with my family and began to work out of my
home as an editor for *Mothering*. In a Cinderella-like story, I
was able to buy the magazine from Addie in 1980 with no down
payment and monthly payments from the magazine. My first
editorial appeared in issue XV, and I wrote an editorial in every
issue thereafter. At first, it was just two columns, a few hundred
words. Over time, I had more to say and crowded more and
more words into the space. Finally, in the 1980s, contributing
editor Gail Grenier Sweet suggested that I give myself more
room for my editorial. At first I gave myself a page, then another.

Today my editorial is two and a third pages, just under 2,000 words.

My editorials have given me such a wonderful opportunity to write on a regular basis and to work out important parenting issues. I often write an editorial about something I am struggling with myself or something I am trying to make sense of in society at large. When I divorced I wrote an editorial called "What Do We Do with the Moon?" and when my children first became adults, I wrote one entitled "In Their Hands." Editorials like "In Defense of Nightwaking" and "Instead of Hitting" are about classic issues I revisit again and again.

Even though I revisit important issues in my essays, I have become more discreet over time. I've become more reluctant over the years to reveal personal details of my children's lives out of respect for them. When they were babies I wrote about them frequently, often by name. Because of this, readers often feel as if they know my children. "We watched you grow up," they will say to them. My writing changed, however, after I happened to overhear the daughter of one of our authors at a conference. She was paging through a recent *Mothering* as she spoke to her friend. "Don't you just hate it when they write about you," she said to her friend.

I realized when I heard that young girl that I was going to have to change the way I wrote and spoke about my children as they grew older. I found that they were especially sensitive during the teen years. My oldest child read an editorial I had written on trusting teens, threw down the magazine, and stomped off as she proclaimed, "You don't trust us!"

Despite the occasional invasion of privacy, my children are proud of my editorials and intrigued that people know them from reading the magazine over the years. You will notice as you read these essays how the topics deepen. I have had the opportunity to return to classic topics over and over again, and in so doing I hope I have been able to refine my understanding and my arguments.

One thing I have learned through writing regular essays is that the hardest part is simply finding your point of view. Once I know my point of view, I can construct the writing and follow the mechanics, but getting to the heart of the matter is the essence of writing. Getting to the heart of the matter requires the willingness to tell the truth. As Willa Cather said, "Artistic growth is, more than it is anything else, a refining of the sense of truthfulness."

It is hard to tell the truth unless you know what you want to tell the truth about. People often ask me how I decide what topic to write on. It's usually easy, often right in front of me. It may be what everyone is talking about, or something in the news or perhaps a classic issue that needs revisiting. Often my editorial will be inspired by some recent real-life event. Sometimes I'll write an editorial with a specific person in mind.

Often that specific person is myself. I think that my greatest strength is that I'm also a reader of the magazine, and I'm living these experiences along with the other readers. In addition, I have had the privilege to hear stories from thousands of parents through letters and conversations.

So many of your stories, like mine, are about following your own way despite discouragement. I encourage others to believe in their creative ideas and dreams because I know from my own experience that success is largely perseverance.

Perseverance is rewarded in parenting as well. There's something about just doing a task over and over again that makes us better at it. Thank you for allowing me to get better at this. I am especially grateful for your companionship along the way. I hope you enjoy these essays.

—Peggy O'Mara

a good parent

WHEN I WALKED INTO MY HOUSE YESTERDAY and found
the teens snowboarding in the greenhouse, I saw an opportunity to change my point of view. This is new for me. I came to
parenting with a long list of "shoulds." The ideas I had of what
a family *should* be often overshadowed the reality of what was
right in front of me. And when the "should" came up against
the reality, I often blamed myself. Blaming myself was a way
of controlling the situation. Then I could paint it all up in my
mind to look pretty again.

Parenthood is different for me now. I have four children;
three of them are teens. Teens are my favorite people. I have
had experiences with them that I never imagined would happen to me. I have said to myself, "*My* children would never do
that," and they have. I have felt the pull between the side of me
that wants to counsel and protect my children with information and insight and the side that wants to control their behavior out of unreasonable fear for them, pridefulness of what
others may think of me, or fear of my own failure as a parent.

Fears regarding my children or my own failure imply a lack
of trust in life and neglect my history with them. Pridefulness
implies that my children are a *product* of mine rather than
individuals of their own creation. And, most practically, after a
certain age, control no longer works.

Children are not objects. The family is not just a pretty picture. Rather, it is made up of dynamic, growing, and changing
individuals whose behavior cannot be predicted or controlled.

When we impose a fixed image on life and tally up its pro-
ceedings on a scorecard of our own imagination, we strangle
life's vitality and deny its inherent perfectibility. In short, we
lack faith in God when we play God by believing that life
"should" be different than it is.

Recent scientific discoveries attest to the virtue of chaos
in assuring synchronicity. Chaos has a function in the order
of things. The aspects of family life that we find chaotic and
unpredictable are usually the ones we try to control, and it is
reassuring to know that we can trust in the integrity of chaos
rather than do everything in our power to avoid it. Life is
born in chaos. Chaos lies at the root of the creative impulse.
It is by harnessing the chaos of ongoing change that we transform the world again and again.

Clean up your room! Brush your teeth! Messes in the home
are chaos. Cavities from not brushing are chaos. As parents,
we want to teach our children to clean up their messes, brush
their teeth, comb their hair, and wash their hands. We recoil
from our lack of success. How many times do we have to
remind them? A lot! Much to my amazement, I have discovered that my children have both their own tastes and their
own timetables for personal grooming; and while I cannot
ensure their compliance with reminders, at least I know that
someday I will not have to.

What I call a mess is often a creative experiment. Because
I am the one with the agenda and the overview, I care who
cleans it up. The children, lost in the creative moment, have
no concern for the future. We are both right. And while I have
a right to live in a home that reflects my sense of aesthetics, so
too do they. When I take on the challenge of reminding with
humor, I acknowledge that children—like the rest of us—take
time to develop new habits and sometimes need help. When I
blame them for forgetting what is yet of little value to them, I
assume laziness that simply does not exist. My daughter has a
habit of falling asleep on the couch. I almost always wake her
up to go upstairs. Once, I turned off the light without waking
her up, and she said, sleepily, "You're supposed to wake me up
and tell me to go upstairs." Another part of the job description.

At my son's school, we talked about the difference in focus between seventh and eighth graders. Whew! Not just *my* kids! Comes with the territory.

It also comes with the territory during the early teen years to go through a Black Phase. It's like the transition phase of birth played out on an adolescent stage. It's the pain of the birth of the self's ensoulment. Of all times in parenthood, this one requires the greatest faith. A child whom you knew intimately becomes a stranger. The values that you shared are up for review. The behavior and dress reflect both an acute self-absorption and an extreme lack of confidence. Parents who don't yet know better, take the behavior personally. Then both parents and teen become lost in the woods.

My son was *really* lost in the woods recently. He was found by a bloodhound named Miss Marple and a team of 60 intrepid rescuers, after spending 15 hours in the woods with four friends and a dog. He and his friends did everything right. The rescuers did everything right. Everything turned out fine. I, however, was lost in the woods of my mind for weeks afterward. The children did not understand what could have happened to them; the parents carried that awareness. The umbilical chord between parent and child is a loop of energy that connects us through the vagaries of life. Whether it be the unexpected accident or the unexpected behavior typical of the Black Phase, we are tied to riding the waves together, and we ride better in the water of real experience than on the shore watching.

Divorce also deserves review in this regard. We hold a collective belief in the tragedy of divorce. We assume that a child's happiness depends on the relationship *between* mother and father rather than on the relationship *with* mother and father. And we ignore the possibility that children of divorce will more deeply understand the commitment of marriage. Divorce underscores the evolution of marriage from a social contract to a personal commitment. The phenomenon of divorce has taught us all that human relationships are fragile works of everyday design, that putting your heart on the line does more to preserve marriage than duty ever could.

Only when we stop in our tracks and drop down into our hearts can we realize that the picture is often bigger than we think. Divorce purifying marriage, the Black Phase of the teen years purifying the young adult, the passion of the young parent's umbilical chord purifying the child's recklessness—all these imply a larger picture that extends beyond our peculiar comforts, our sense of pride and accomplishment, or our longings for predictability.

Life is not static. We can't just get a fix on it and walk away. When it looks different from what we expect, it may still be what we need. Although conflict with our loved ones does not go away once we accept the virtue of chaos, when we stop blaming ourselves or taking our children's behavior personally—most of the time—we have the chance to meet as real people in the depth of our individuality, where we can escape personal isolation and resolve conflict from a place of ongoing mutual regard.

In the November 14, 1991, issue of *Rolling Stone*, Matthew Fox mentions that his mother had seven children in 11 years and still took two hours for herself every day. Not my original idea of a good parent. Now, I wouldn't be one *without* time for myself. He speaks, too, of our birthright of joy. "What does God do all day?" Matt asks. "She enjoys herself." He speaks also of traditional peoples, who experience more joy in a day than we do in a year. They are lost in the moment rather than worried about being contradicted by it.

More joy! What does life look like, what does family life look like, when we meet it with joy rather than despair? What if we were really meant to be happy, and it's up to us to experience the joy? What if it's all about putting our hearts on the line? What if it's all about going dancing more?

From Mothering, *issue no. 62 (Winter 1992).*

taking a chance on life

LIFE IS A MYSTERY PLAY. It is not a plot conveniently
scripted by Hollywood screenwriters. It does not have a predictable timeline with mood pieces sporadically interwoven.
It *is* a mood piece. It is much richer, deeper, and more complex than we might have imagined, and thus we often miss it
altogether.

We miss it altogether when we live someone else's script
for us instead of living the authentic life of our own design.
We fail to notice that while we are making plans for life, life
may have something else entirely in mind for us. We live life
either as though it has an inherent wisdom of its own or as
though we have to invent one for it.

When we live life as though it has inherent wisdom, as
though God is everywhere and in everything, we take risks.
When we believe that we ascribe meaning to life, that there
is no one greater than ourselves, we must keep things under
control because there is no safety net.

Risk taking itself is endangered in our society. Point of
view has been co-opted by special interests, advertising, and
economics. A great conformity has come to our times. Those
of us who are willing to take risks are in service to the preser-
vation of life itself.

Vitality for life is manifested in the fire of passion. Passion
for life translates into a *presence in life*, a *showing up* that
takes risks because it cannot do otherwise. All of life becomes
a love affair, full of emotional charge. The areas most charged
with the passion of the moment and the ongoing paradox of

conditional and unconditional love are those of relationship. Relationship with ourselves and others: love, parenting, birth, and the creative process.

Relationships with others are always changing, and while we expect them to go smoothly, relationships by their nature deepen our consciousness often through transformative suffering. It is our fear of suffering that keeps us from the authentic life. In the authentic life, suffering is the fuel of personal change.

We suffer in love, in birth, in parenting, in art. We suffer in life. And from suffering comes the willingness to surrender to the ecstatic nature of life. The true nature of life is that it is a continual and ongoing process of birth, death, and rebirth.

In birth, it is this fear of suffering that leads women to see their bodies only as vehicles and to devalue the transformational experience of birth. Thus they choose drugs and interventions; having already separated their minds from their bodies, they will then find it possible to separate themselves from their babies. The institutionalized birth rituals in hospitals ensure that women will objectify their bodies and make choices that put the outcome of birth in the hands of technology and the ownership of the baby in the hands of society.

Birth is in and of itself a rite of passage, and as such, wherever it occurs, it will produce its own set of rituals. The hospital rituals produce and increase dependency on technology and technicians, while rituals at home create the home as sacred space receptive to the needs of the mother and as source of her empowerment.

The passionate presence of the birth energy is more compatibly managed at home, where unpredictability can be welcomed, than at the hospital, where control of events and conformity of experience mark the institution's effectiveness. Hospital birth assumes that risks can be controlled. Thus, when something goes wrong, someone must be blamed, because technology guarantees safety. Homebirth assumes that risk is inherent in birth. If homebirth is safe—and it is—then we have to accept that risk is inherent in life. To believe that homebirth is safe is to challenge our basic cultural belief system.

To undermine our basic cultural belief system is to live the authentic life. We who create a belief system out of our own unfolding lives will create the future. We can no longer evaluate our experiences by how they conform to the fairy tale. We have to ask ourselves how challenged, inspired, and present we feel in life; what has heart and meaning; where hope is. Success is the raw and tender feeling of life lived in the moment—not the pretty picture.

Unfortunately, we are in the habit of measuring successes by quantity not quality. While we spend more money than any other country on health care, we have poor statistics on infant mortality and cesarean birth. In less than 20 years, our cesarean rate has increased from 5 percent to 23 percent. Babies in 19 other countries have a smaller chance of being born by cesarean than babies in the US. Twenty-three countries have better infant mortality statistics than the US. A baby born in Hong Kong has a 33 percent greater chance of living to his or her first birthday than does a baby born in the US. We're pedaling faster and going slower.

In the same way that control of the natural process of birth does not improve upon it, controlling children does not improve upon them. One can either connect with one's children, trust that they have unique and individual timetables for healthy development, and become an expert in observing and then assessing their needs, or one can separate from one's children, prescribe appropriate behavior for them to follow, and seek help from experts outside of oneself.

Trust assumes that wisdom is inherent in life. Control assumes that wisdom is outside of personal experience. These two threads struggle for dominance in our psyches and in our society. Our political debates over abortion, daycare, welfare, midwifery, and the cause of the LA riots are really about trust versus control. They all underline the same question: Can we trust life or not?

Birth is about as safe as life gets. Life is about as safe as life gets. We can wear safety helmets, eliminate diving boards, strap ourselves in airplanes and automobiles, and make the world one big air bag—and still life will happen to us. Life will pulse on, more powerful and more unpredictable than we can imagine.

Life is like sailing. Sometimes the wind catches us and runs with us. Sometimes we're steady in calm water. Sometimes the wind comes up unexpectedly. Choosing our tack as we go, and keeping just at the edge of the wind, we are neither at the mercy of the wind nor in control of it.

Children drive us crazy in modern society because they are so alive. We can't control them. They are irrepressible, unsocialized, and reminiscent of the way we feel when we are most alive. In a society that values straight lines, antiseptic conditions, and standardized care, children continually surprise and upset us. Institutionalizing children at earlier and earlier ages ensures that they will be controlled as soon as possible.

We live in contracted times, and it is in such times that society needs art most. The source of creative expression; the fuel for the authentic life, for the suffering and the resurrection of transformation cannot easily be tolerated by those who do not value emotional experience. Just as in a sterile society, few risk peer censure for authentic life experiences, so do few risk emotional angst for authentic creative expression. Likewise, fewer and fewer women value the suffering of birth as a transformative experience. Birth is not just about the birth of the baby. It is about the birth of the mother.

The authentic life continually gives birth to itself. The parent's love for the child renews the life of the parent. Valuing immersion in life over protection from it allows one to make difficult and lonely choices. Birth choices, parenting commitments, love and partnership, artistic integrity—all are political in our times. Each assumes that the individual *can know*. Each assumes that life can be trusted. Each assumes that life itself is the safety net. Society conspires against such faith at the same time it depends upon it for survival.

From Mothering, *issue no. 64 (Summer 1992).*

softer shades of gray

YESTERDAY I LOOKED THROUGH OLD PHOTO ALBUMS with a friend who did not know me when the pictures were taken. I had borne three babies and gained 50 pounds since then. Surprised at how much birthing had changed my body, I judged myself and my attractiveness. I was expecting to show my friend how much I had changed and how much better I looked now. Instead, I found that my past self looked beautiful to me.

I feel beautiful now for the first time in my life. Looking back at myself as a young mother, I see that I was also beautiful then, in the many shapes and sizes my body wore over the years. It was not better then, nor is it better now. I have space to believe in both past and present, even though sometimes they appear contradictory.

This is new for me. I have been accustomed, as many of us are, to putting things in black and white boxes, compartmentalizing to create emotional safety. I find that the softer, subtle shades of gray appeal to me now. Life is many things at once. I no longer want to think in "either/or" terms.

Spiritual maturity is the ability to endure paradox. If paradox means that which is contradictory, then parenting surely takes the cake.

I never imagined that the baby I wanted so much would grow up and leave home. Just as her birth was a rite of passage, so too is her leaving. In fact, I am undergoing a rite of passage through the experience of my two daughters. This fall, my oldest, who began formal schooling in ninth grade, will enter college, and my youngest will enter school for the first time in fifth grade. I enjoyed homeschooling for many years, and I believe that it gave my children a wonderful foundation for imagination and intellectual growth. I am also glad that they are now in school, because this, too, suits their needs. As one daughter leaves home for college and the other enters school for the first time, I feel *sad* and I feel free. Both feelings belong, and neither one cancels out the other. Emotions are not black and white.

When parents are young and marriage is new, the baby can become the carrier of the parents' black and white projections. Many of us find that the needs of the baby contradict our own needs. Often we compartmentalize ourselves and nourish only the parent self, hoping to pick up the pieces of our other selves later.

While there are certainly times when the needs of the baby are greater than those of the adult, the needs of the parent do not have to be sacrificed to the needs of the baby. Nor do the needs of the baby have to be sacrificed for the needs of the parent. What is needed to balance this situation is strategy, not sacrifice.

Looking back on my life as a young parent, I did not know it was possible to achieve this balance. I knew only how to give. My own self-esteem was supported by the belief that giving to others was all that was really valuable. I now know the cost of spending too much of myself. Giving more than you can afford in the name of love is not love. The fact that the needs of the parent and the needs of the baby sometimes contradict each other does not mean they can't coexist.

I hear so often about the lives of lovers who become parents. Marriage is a cauldron of self-growth, and babies turn up the heat. **He:** "What happened to my lover? She hasn't wanted to make love since the baby was born." **She:** "I'm all touched out, my hormones are on hold, and I have no idea whose body this is anymore." **He:** "I'm freaked out by her new body; it's hard to see her as my lover when I think of her as a mother." **She:** "I don't think he finds me attractive anymore. Everything has changed so much. I need *time* with him and some love and affection." **He:** "I come home after a long day, and she has an agenda for me. I just want to relax and catch my breath. If she needs help, I'd like her to tell me what she needs without any judgment." **She:** "I don't understand why he can't see that I need help. I sit all day with the baby and don't get anything done. I want him to see what needs to get done. I don't want to tell him." **He:** "She's always upset." **She:** "He's so angry."

Sound familiar? I sometimes wonder if all this talking about, figuring out, and analyzing "the relationship" doesn't suck the romance out of it. Maybe it's not about the baby. Maybe it's about growing up ourselves. Maybe it's that we take ourselves too seriously without taking our needs at all seriously. When we take ourselves seriously, we think a lot about our lives; when we take our needs seriously, we do something about them. Taking our needs seriously requires that we find some time alone and some time together as a couple *on a regular basis.* Love is like a rose. It doesn't just wait around on the stem, hoping you'll get back to it. Either it blossoms, it begins to get brown around the edges from insufficient water, or it never opens at all.

I do not advocate prolonged separations from babies. I do see, however, that the inability to find *any* time for ourselves or our marriages is not always because of the baby's needs but because of our own unfulfilled needs that we project onto the baby.

Marriage itself is a paradox. A good marriage can come to an end. A bad marriage can go on for a lifetime. Who's to say? Marriage is not an end itself. It supports and mirrors the process of individuation. Our job is to continually become more of who we are. Unfortunately, we may strive to continually become more than who we are.

When we model sacrifice and domination of one person's needs over another's, we do not teach our children love. Love teaches joy, and it is possible to create families where all needs are equal. When all needs are equal, there is no shame. Families with unfulfilled needs create continual crises to get these needs met. And the unfulfilled needs of the parents become the legacy to their children.

I am totally attached to my children, and I can let them go. I can respond to their needs as well as take care of my own. I will always see them as my babies, and I can learn to be with them adult to adult. I can continue to love them even as I let them go. I can bring both softness and strength to my parenting. And I can give myself up to love without giving myself away to it.

Being an adult, being a partner, being a friend, being a parent—all challenge us to live in the paradox of the creative moment rather than to live in the illusion of control. I do not have to make the old me bad to make the new me good. I do not have to abandon the tenets of homeschooling to incorporate formal schooling into my children's lives. I do not have to deny my own needs to respond to the needs of those I love. All are valuable. Always there are leaves *and* roots. Always there is chaos *and* order. Always there is anger. Always there is the way of the open heart . . . melody *and* rhythm.

From Mothering, *issue no. 65 (Fall 1992).*

it ain't over yet

LAST FALL, MY OLDEST DAUGHTER WENT TO COLLEGE. And she came back. I didn't know—I thought that maybe at 18, they grew up and left home. No. It ain't over yet. This has turned out to be one of my most profound experiences. As with my daughter's birth, her college experience turned me 180 degrees so that everything looked quite different and I felt, as I did after her birth, that no one had *really* told me what to expect.

When we prepared for college, we did all the right things. My daughter took the college entrance tests and pored over books listing the numerous college choices. I went to college meetings at her high school, waded through financial aid options, and made lists of college supplies. In effect, I got the boiling water and the chord clamps ready yet forgot to talk about the pain. We spoke a great deal about the practical details and little about the potential emotional realities. Fortunately, this time around, we're a family who has learned how to talk about the pain and how to handle the unexpected.

My daughter chose a large college because she had attended a small, private high school. She chose a college town she liked that is less than 500 miles from home and where we have old family friends. She chose a college that has versatility of course offerings. And although none of her friends planned to go there, she visited the campus beforehand and liked it. She made a good choice.

The reality of life away from home turned out to be very different from the widely accepted fantasy of college. The

reality was a large institution with many of a large institution's
pitfalls. We place our young adults in a new situation that
carries heavy personal, societal, and financial expectations of
success. To support them in this new and important venture,
we pull the rug out from under their personal lives. They leave
family and friends—their existing support network—to live
with someone they've never met, in a room so small that furniture must be stacked. The room has one window that looks
out on the roof. The bathroom is down the hall. The food is
cafeteria-style.

For young people who want to leave their present situation, who are highly motivated to learn or pursue a career, or
who are of a different temperament, such experiences may
not be sacrifices. However, for those who value aesthetic and
emotional experience, large college life may be too impersonal.
I am surprised that campus life cannot be more responsive to
the individual person.

At her first dorm meeting, my daughter was given a piece
of candy, a condom, and a black whistle. The whistle was in
case of threatened rape, and stiff penalties were attached to
irresponsible whistle blowing. It was rumored that a student
whose roommate commits suicide receives all As for the
semester. Amid the innuendos suggesting serious emotional
experiences, very little acknowledgment was given to the
day-to-day coping with these new situations. Parents were
cautioned to hold a hard line when they received "the call"
from their child asking to come home.

The profundity of it all came in contemplating this hard
line. Unlike the period following my daughter's birth, this time
I had the memory of my own college experience and knew
how much my own responses to her would realign the choices
I had made as a young adult. While I encouraged her to give
herself time to adjust, it quite frankly did not turn out to be
my line to hold.

For one thing, I have the habit of trusting my daughter and
her perception of her own experience. She knew when she
wanted to walk, to talk, to wean, to go to school. Her choices
have been just fine so far. I have had no reason to distrust her
experience—and neither has she. Once my daughter decided

she did not want to stay at this college, she had no ambivalence, no second thoughts, no looking back. She simply knew
her own mind.

She had no guilt either. Once she made sure that I would
receive a tuition and housing refund, she was free of concerns. Having never been lonely, she could make no sense of
unnecessary loneliness. Her large classes did not cause her to
complain; what she could not endure was the abrupt loss of
her family and a social life that had been working well for her.

Due to her ability to know so clearly what she wanted, and
my ability to trust her feelings even though they were not
my plans, my entire life fell into place in a different way. If it
is really true that someone can be trusted to understand her
own experiences, make her own choices, and take responsibility for her own decisions, then it must be possible to fashion
very unique lives for ourselves—lives that are truly handmade,
rather than imitations of transitory societal standards of
behavior.

My daughter made all of the times I had toughed it out the
sadnesses they really were, rather than the necessities I had
believed them to be. Her decision made my whole body relax,
as I no longer had to be ever-alert to the "right way." Her clarity demonstrated that it *is* possible to raise children who know
and trust their inner experience, who have not been lied to,
who are not neurotic.

They have a name for what my daughter is doing. It is
called taking a year off. When I went to college, there was no
education to speak of, and women who didn't go to college
right after high school usually did not go to college at all. This
is no longer so. My daughter is seriously examining the college
options right in her own backyard, with the knowledge that
she can return to a larger school when she's ready to specialize.

Surprisingly, many of her former classmates are choosing
similar paths. Several boys went to a university nearby so that
they could be together and close to home. Others have come
home. Some would like to. A few are traveling. And certainly,
many are adjusting to college life just fine.

Like birth, college requires us to prepare as best we can,
knowing that we must also be able to respond to the unex-

pected. In our family, we value personal timetables, connection, communication, cooperation, and support for one another. We share difficult emotions and hard times. In our family, how someone feels is very important. Our quality of life is very important to all of us. And so it is with my daughter and her classmates. They have broken the mold of "ivy league" expectations and recognized at a young age that life is not only about going after something, but it is also about getting there. These students are insisting on getting there in the style to which they have become accustomed.

From Mothering, *issue no. 66 (Spring 1993).*

the courage to divorce

I WOULD LIKE TO REFUTE the popular misconception that divorce is an act of cowardice, a running away, an easy way out. It is, in fact, a great act of courage when it has as its motivation the continued growth and health of the family. It is an open invitation to a hurricane. It is a purposefully chosen healing crisis.

My children are not from a "broken home." They have two homes. They dislike going back and forth and living in two houses, yet neither of their homes is broken. My marriage did not fail. It ended. The self-inflicted natural disaster of divorce changes many lives irrevocably. It is painful, embarrassing, depressing, exhausting, and often expensive. I do not believe that anyone who was not severely oppressed psychologically, physically, or spiritually would choose it.

I am certain that both people in any marriage are equally responsible for what happens in that marriage, and though one may look like the "bad guy" or one may call the alarm, both are responsible. The bitter predivorce and postdivorce bickering that often ensues is an expression of the toxic underbelly of the unresolved and unspoken oppression and suffering of the marriage. As you marry, so you divorce.

After the marriage ends, the subtle values underlying the relationship are more overtly expressed. The "old" couple can either continue their suffering into a postdivorce relationship or choose to relate in a new way. For the sake of the children, they can transform the loss of the marriage and let it go.

I do not believe anymore—although I did throughout most of my life—that all children are mightily harmed by divorce. I know that some are more resilient to change than others. My younger children, who had few if any preconceptions about divorce, had an easier time than my older ones, who were aware of the stigma of divorce and afraid that their parents' divorce would be as ugly as those they has heard about from their friends.

Curiously, I am from a generation that has coined the terms *dysfunctional family*, *recovery*, and *inner child* after growing up with parents who stayed together for the children, who stayed together no matter what. Many children of "intact" families are harmed not by divorce but by a divorce that should have happened and didn't.

In measuring the impact of divorce, it is difficult to distinguish between the many factors involved. There is parental separation, death of the idea of the family, fear of physical separation, violence or rage that may have existed in the home prior to the divorce, as well as tension and disharmony that existed prior to divorce—all of which have their individual effects.

It is important to appreciate that families who are able to recover from the pain and disappointment of divorce can indeed be healthy and happy families again and can even be *healthier* families. This does not mean that I encourage divorce or that I believe the positive qualities of divorce will drive hordes to the divorce courts. *We are better than that!* We *do not* give up easily.

In fact, most of us wait *too long* to divorce, and we end up suffering the pain of predivorce withdrawal and alienation in addition to the pain of postdivorce bickering. The point is that whether we wait too long or not, divorce is a tragedy. It is a tragedy because it couldn't have happened any other way.

We know from anthropological studies that in hunter-gatherer societies, serial relationships were correlated to the vulnerable first few years of a human infant's life. Lifetime mating was correlated to the needs of the agricultural and industrial societies in more recent times. Human beings are adaptive. We may now be adapting to yet another change in human mating patterns.

For the first time in history, human beings do not have to marry for money, property, social status, safety, or the legitimacy of children. We're new at this relationship stuff. We're new at communicating honestly as men and women. The word *communication* was not even mentioned in the marital world until the 1950s.

One scientist suggests that alienation in marriage begins with contempt and that contempt arises when one partner becomes flooded with the other's negative emotions. Sometimes we can learn new ways to express negative emotions. Sometimes we are incompatible. We can be compatible with someone at one time in our lives and not at others. We love some people for short periods of time. We love some people for long periods of time.

John Welwood, in his book *Journey of the Heart*, speaks eloquently about the challenging path of true love. Many of us marry without realizing what marriage is or what it requires in terms of personal compatibility. Many of us marry for lust, for our church, for our parents, for our society, for our ideas of the pretty picture. Some of us go on to divorce because, ironically enough, marriage has given us the comfort to discover our true selves, who, much to our own dismay and disappointment, may have something else entirely in mind for us.

Marriage is about a bond to a larger society, a public statement of intent. Love, the foundation of marriage, is magic. As such, love cannot be analyzed or understood by the intellect. As Kahlil Gibran says in *The Prophet*, "Think not that you can direct the path of love. If love finds you worthy, he will direct your path."

By the same token, divorce never makes sense to the mind. It only makes sense to the heart.

I had the good fortune of meeting Kenny Loggins and his wife Julia Loggins some time ago. We spoke of the courage of divorce. In his album *Leap of Faith*, Kenny sings poignantly of leaving his first marriage. Explaining to his children why he had to leave the marriage, he sings, "Love should teach you joy. Not the imitation that your mommy and daddy tried to show you."

When love dies in a marriage and cannot be revived, it does not teach joy. It teaches hardship, disappointment, and withdrawal. This false impression of love does not give children a true model of love to aspire to later on in life. As adults, they may keep duplicating the false love, believing—because it was all they ever saw as children—that it is true love. This is a greater tragedy than divorce.

I am impressed by the divorced parents in my community. Many continue to function as partners in parenting. They consult with each other on child-related matters and attend the same school functions, sometimes even sitting together. More and more of my friends are finding their way through the pain of divorce to the other side. More and more have learned to tolerate each other's personal limitations and to develop a coparenting relationship that is cooperative although no longer intimate.

I do not like to fill out forms that include "divorced" as a choice. I do not define myself by what I no longer am. I would suggest that we hurt ourselves as much by the stigma of divorce and our preconceptions of it as by its reality. Perhaps adults and children who are hurt by divorce are hurt even more by feelings of failure and disappointment that stem from the collective belief that divorce is someone's fault. Making it someone's fault implies that it could have been avoided. Most often, it cannot.

I believe that if we as a society increase compassion for divorce while committing ourselves as individuals to decreasing blame and shame within ourselves and our relationships, we will begin to heal the stigma of divorce. Along with the healing will come the openness in which healthy marriages can really thrive and new, healthier marriages can be born after divorce.

I have a garden. In my garden, I planted two perennials side by side—two beautiful companion plants. Some years went by, and the plants grew strong and healthy next to each other. They grew, however, at different rates. In time, one began to grow bigger and bushier than the other, crowding the other out. The other ceased to thrive. I have two choices: I can leave them where they are and let the other lead a diminished life at best, or die at worst, or I can transplant the other so that they will both have the soil, water, and sunlight needed for growth. Perennials are hardy. They come back bigger and stronger year after year. Sometimes they need to be transplanted.

In my greenhouse is an orchid, a beautiful and fragrant flower, and yet my greenhouse is too hot for it. If I leave the orchid there, it will scorch around the edges, lose its beautiful scent, and eventually wither and die. My parsley, on the other hand, thrives in the heat. It grows full and bushy as long as it gets enough water. In winter, however, it will grow long and spindly, looking for the light. There is nothing wrong with the orchid or the parsley. Each one simply needs the right conditions in order to thrive and reach its full potential.

We are all like plants—blood and chlorophyll have nearly identical compositions. Sometimes we grow strong and hardy in the same soil we were planted in at birth. Other times, our birth soil is dry and sandy, and we must struggle for survival; and through struggling, we become hardy. Sometimes we transplant ourselves into unfavorable soil because we don't yet know our ideal conditions for growth. Other times, the soil we have transplanted ourselves into and thrived in for years no longer suits us. And sometimes we must transplant ourselves bare root by our own volition to ensure that the entire garden will continue to grow and thrive.

It would be nice if we could be kinder to ourselves and others about divorce.

From Mothering, *issue no. 68 (Fall 1993).*

hearth and home

A WOMAN SITS ALONE in the middle of the night with a crying baby. She feels unequal to the task of being a mother and is stretched almost to her breaking point. Yet she carries on. In the morning, things look better.

A man rocks his wakeful daughter. She is tired. He is tired. He is losing patience and about to explode with anger. He takes a breath. She falls asleep. In the morning, things look better.

This magazine is for that woman. It is for that man. I hope our articles and dialogue inform, inspire, and support you as a parent, as a person. Articles that may seem to proselytize a point of view are, in fact, intended for that one man or that one woman. In lieu of wrapping us all up in a big blanket for a long nap, I hope to offer "word food" to get you through the night.

We publish articles on the downside of vaccination, for example, not to tell those who love vaccinations to give them up but to provide parents who are making the vaccination decision with responsible, well-researched information on the subject. We publish articles on the attachment process not to provoke guilt—we all have enough of that to go around—but to help move the national debate around child care beyond economics. And I write editorials about compassion for divorce not to encourage divorce but to provide support.

With so much flux in our society, with natural disasters, national disputes, worries about money, and not enough time, we "parents in the trenches" need help. At the same time, our response to society's fluctuations will determine which outmoded customs and mores are to be changed and which biological imperatives are to be protected from change.

When *Mothering* was started in 1976, motherhood was held in disdain. Women were expanding into the workplace, and motherhood was getting a bum rap. While the notion of mother as family servant needed to change, the importance of motherhood needed to be preserved. Since the seventies, women as well as men have become disenchanted with the material world and aware of its limitations. Now, while society is going mad with materialism, individuals and families are just as madly trying to figure out how to live in tune with their personal values.

Over the years, *Mothering* has focused attention on the importance of hearth and home. New medical studies verify the importance of long leisurely meals for overall health. People need one another, need to feel connected to one another and to spend time with loved ones. When we do not have enough time for the ones we love we become sick at heart. Babies and children, it seems, are perfect guides for reconnecting to this real life of the heart.

Children come into the world from the past and the future at the same time. They are equipped genetically to be part of the future, yet they are produced by the evolutionary past. They are molded not by current social trends but by millions of years of evolution. They contain the biological imperative of our species, and they come to tell us what that is. They tell us what they need by their emotional response to life. And if we follow their cues, we not only create an environment for their happiness but also learn how to live better ourselves.

Children can help us see a benign universe. While advertising and media bombardments paint a picture of an out-of-control world that we must control in order to feel safe, children and nature tell a different story. Colin Turnbull, who has lived with the Pygmies, reports that they have a benign worldview. They believe that they are protected. They believe that the forests will meet their need for foods, shelter, and spiritual protection. They believe that they are taken care of. They feel at one with their environment, in a relationship of

love and respect born of a positive attitude toward the feminine. Imagine how it would feel to totally trust life. Children
already know how. They see the world as a safe place. They see
the world as a sacred place.

Believing in a benign universe is no easy task. It is like
breathing in and out at the same time. Our belief must fuel
the change at the same time that we become the change. And
although our children every day remind us how simple and
beautiful life really is, this picture is difficult to see when our
lives are oppressed by worry or want. That is why real family
support in this society must go beyond the partisan bickering
and self-righteous moralizing of recent years. We can hold
onto an ideal for the family at the same time we have compassion for all. We could then get the homeless off the streets
instead of wondering if they are to blame. We could address
quality child care and admit to the importance of the attachment process. And we could let Baby Jessica decide who her
parents are.

Life is more than analyses, weights, measures, and legal
precedents. It is more than fancy things and chocolate chip
cookies. It is about the slow blue flame that burns in rich and
poor, young and old, and that needs stoking to stay alive. It's
about appreciating the essential renewal that family, nature,
home, and hearth provide—and protecting each one as a
national resource.

Protecting the home and the hearth begins with understanding what helps and what hurts families. All families are
hurt by the low social status of parenthood. Families are hurt
by consumerism, materialism, careerism. Too many demands
on their time also hurt them, as do too many standards of correct behavior and too much demand for conformity.

Unhealthy families are too busy for one another. They have
little interest in and make little effort toward self-improvement.
In unhealthy families, domination rules. Family members
victimize and shame one another. They don't ask for help and
are unpredictable, inconsistent, and insecure.

Healthy families, on the other hand, show appreciation for
one another a great deal. They are dedicated to promoting the
welfare and happiness of each member, and they value the

unity of the family. Healthy families develop good communication skills and spend time talking with one another. They
talk about everything. They also spend large quantities of time
together. Healthy families share a sense of a greater good or
power in life—a belief that creates strength and purpose. They
view stress as an opportunity to grow, and they ask for help.
Healthy families can bounce back from anger, too.

Knowing more about healthy and unhealthy families helps
us focus on *traits* rather than demographics, political beliefs,
or economic status as signs of well-being. Knowing more
about these traits helps us appreciate the importance of
hearth and home and seek protection for it within a rapidly
changing society. Protecting the family means that we
recognize the importance of the early years of imprinting in
human families.

Recently, I saw a baby seal stranded on a beach. Everyone
knew not to touch the baby. Everyone knew that something sensitive was going on between the seal baby and the
seal mother, something that could be easily disturbed. Hardly
anyone knows that human infancy and the roots of the human
family are just as sensitive.

We are born experiencing touch, intimacy, breastfeeding,
and physical contact; and we are raised to fear bodily contact.
Could adult obsession with sexuality be related to repres-
sions in childhood? Could violence in society be related to
an impairment of conscience during the attachment process?
Surely we compromise the capacity to love and be loved, to
be intimate and trusting, by underestimating the importance
and effects of too much stress on the family unit.

The life of the hearth and home is contradictory to the
busyness of modern materialistic society. It is less, slower,
simpler. It is sitting and reading. It is the fireplace. Meals
together. Board games. Going to the movies. Taking walks.
Watering the garden. Doing nothing. Brunch. Watching the
sunset. Lying in the hammock. These things are not frivolous;
they are essential. They are the foundation. They are the roots.
They are sacred time. All expansion into the world requires
times of contraction, times of doing nothing.

The hearth and the home. The fire in the belly can be stirred up by kind words that encourage, information that is helpful, a home environment that is warm and cozy, family habits that support unity. Quite frankly, every family I see already knows this and wants it. We're in the process of dismantling a society that won't support hearth and home at the same time we are re-creating one that will. Looks like a meltdown. Might just be a birth.

Some say the earth was created when Our Mother was menstruating and Our Father was crying. Something in us must die in order be born. It helps to be in frequent contact with the underbelly, the richness of hearth and home that sustains us despite the changes throughout the world and within ourselves.

We're all looking for some good news. Hoping for a miracle. Wishing it would all be over fast. Get done with the fixing. Maybe there's no guy coming on a white horse. Maybe there's no guy coming on a black one either. Whenever the world is too much, I go outside or look at the garden or the clouds. Or I climb upstairs to my room, sit on my bed, and look out the window. Sometimes my kids come up and sit on the bed, and we talk. Our fears come up, and we talk about them. We work them out. I hope our culture is re-creating a world that has time for these moments to happen. In the meantime, I'll make up my own . . . here at home.

From Mothering, *issue no. 69 (Winter 1993).*

some important things to remember

WHEN MY FIRST CHILD WAS BORN, I marveled at the fact that no one had told me how amazing and transformative it is to birth a baby. No one had hinted at the power of the experience, and I wondered what else about motherhood would be more than it appeared. Now, 20 years later, as my oldest becomes an adult, I know that much about motherhood is deeper than it seems. I also know that a few essential ideas prove helpful over and over again and hold it all together when nothing else can. These are some of the important things I have learned as my children have been growing up.

I wish someone had told me the truth about labor: that it would hurt, that it would be a big pain, that it wouldn't be worse than an abscessed tooth, and that I would be able to handle it. Maybe no one could have told me that. Maybe that is the lesson I could have learned only from birth itself. Nonetheless, 20 years ago we lied to ourselves. We called contractions "rushes," which they certainly are, yet in our attempt to appreciate the natural experience of birth and not be afraid of it, we couched the power of the experience in meager words and added to the fear of the unknown.

Not until I had given birth twice did I really believe that birth was safe and that my pregnant body was normal. That learning came from experience. And after birthing four children, I learned that an inherent integrity of the body serves women well during childbirth and that most women, unencumbered with excessive technological intervention, birth normally. In addition to being amazing and transformative, birth is inherently safe and normal.

Just as birth taught me to trust my innate physical integrity, motherhood has taught me to trust my children's innate emotional integrity. Although I was prepared to believe in this integrity from my previous experience with children, as a new parent, I had to build confidence in myself to really appreciate my children's needs and wants, even as I accommodated them. I accommodated them because it made sense to me that their needs and wants were the same, but I had experience only in unequal relationships and I had to learn to live with my children in true mutual regard.

Learning to live in true mutual regard becomes possible after developing an appropriate sense of separation from your child. By this, I do not mean a separation in which you distance yourself emotionally from your child and do not perceive, address, or meet your child's needs. I'm talking about a separation that allows you to respond to your child's needs without taking responsibility for your child's emotional experience. In some ways, we parents are mere companions, unable, even in the best of circumstances, to control our child's experiences. And it is this uncontrollable nature of life that keeps it engaging.

I learned from my children that they had a right to their feelings and that the rough spots in growing up, like the pain of birth, go with the territory. As an older parent, I know that I have a lifetime of moments with my children. I can make mistakes, be less than loving at times. My children will not be ruined. We will reconcile. After spending much of my early parenthood avoiding conflict or dramatically demanding its immediate and peaceful resolution, I now appreciate that the task of the family is to teach conflict-resolving skills and that one can learn these only from conflict. The true key to resolving conflict is wanting to reconcile more than wanting to be right.

Wanting to reconcile with my children gave me the opportunity to really be myself with them. In appreciating our children's vulnerability, we often give them more than we want to, and by doing so we develop unrealistic expectations of attention in them and a stream of resentment in ourselves. Sometimes as new parents we are disingenuous with our children, playing with them when we don't want to, letting them help with dinner when we don't have the time.

It used to frighten me to set limits with my children. I believed a good parent was ever available to her children. I believed I could ruin them. I also feared that if I did not respond to their needs in the moment, I never would. In truth, children need clear knowledge about the limits of human interaction. Just as they learn conflict resolution from conflict, so do they learn good personal boundaries by observing and interacting with the good personal boundaries of others.

While we may have strong and "right" opinions as adults, our job is to communicate them to our children as opinions, not facts. We do our children a great disservice when, out of overzealousness or narcissism, we do not allow them to differentiate between fact and opinion. It is our responsibility to tell them the truth about the world. Plain and simple. We can do this because we don't have to be perfect; we just have to be authentic.

As I came to be myself with my children, I had to learn to talk to them in ways that were not hurtful. The very core of my language base had been adversarial, for my language reflected my personal history. My language about conflict inferred that others were out to get me, to attack or hurt me. My experience with my children told me that while I sometimes felt anger in response to their behavior, I had never seen them act malevolently toward me.

What I have learned over many years is to express, as author Haim Ginott says, "nuances of anger without nuances of insult." The way to do this is to talk about myself, my feelings, and my experiences rather than attacking or blaming the other person. This way, I can get angry and crabby and stomp around, experiencing the power of my feelings without hurting anyone else. Other people don't always change after I've shown how I feel. Sometimes I have to change. And even if no one changes, I feel better having expressed myself, because I have taken responsibility for my feelings. This way, it is easier to rebound from anger into the cheerful life of the family.

Much of this new talking came from new thinking that developed in my years as a mother. Having been willing to accept my children's inherent emotional integrity as infants, I was reluctant to begin distrusting them as children. Although cultural messages suggested that children were crafty manipulators, I never experienced an instant in which my children were not operating out of their own, sometimes unfathomable, though very real needs.

The belief that has served me more than all others is this idea of trust. When all else fails, when you are at your wit's end, when you have no idea what is going on, trusting your own gut responses and trusting your child's experience are your only options. It will always get you back to basics, and if there is more to a situation than meets the eye, trusting yourself creates a safe place in which difficult things can come up.

Providing a safety net for the trust is an understanding of the phases and stages that all children, that all of us, continually go through. Nothing about children is written in stone. No one can escape radical change. We go through radical change as our children grow from 21 inches long to 6 feet tall. A lot of stuff happens along the way that no one could have anticipated. When going through radical change, it helps to know that what you see with your own eyes is real.

Knowing that children go through phases and stages can help steel one's patience when an easygoing child seems beset by insufferable behavioral changes. Children go through intense phases because they are laying the foundation for future behavior and learning. It helps to remember that love comes in phases, too, in waves. It ebbs and flows, has peaks and valleys; this is how it carries on, this is its quality. Children's health reveals a similar pattern: illness is often followed by a growth spurt; teeth often erupt after a fussy and feverish spell. Challenging phases and stages often follow and precede delightful phases and stages.

Understanding the nature of phases and stages helps us to see that contraction follows expansion, equalizing behavior and experience. The "terrible twos" top off the dependent baby years. The "sweet threes" counterpoint the twos before

them and the independent fours ahead of them. Children at
five are protective of the personal ground they have gained;
they want to have choices, and they are incapable of waiting.
By seven, the age of reason arrives; children become more
"reasonable" and better able to accommodate others' needs.
At nine, an inner question about God arises; children begin
asking about life and death, expressing fears of the unknown,
and exhibiting unusual attachments to clothing or routines.
The preteen years are a time of ambivalence. No longer young,
not yet old, preteens are somewhat reluctant to grow up and
often vacillate between playing with dolls and "Joes" and call-
ing each other on the phone. The withdrawal in the early teen
years is a reaction to the self-consciousness and self-awareness that emerge between 12 and 15; young teens must review
their acquired values and those of their family so that they can
"rejoin" the family as older teens, sweet and integrated.

Trusting ourselves and our children during these phases
is easier once we accept that children are always changing.
Sometimes the best way to respond to difficult behavior is
simply to watch and wait, aware that it may well "fix" itself
without our intervention. Being a parent can be so much like
playing God that we tend to forget that judging ourselves by
our children's behavior ascribes to us an omnipotence we
simply do not have. With children, it's good enough to be
fallible human beings. In fact, it's essential. Children demand
that we be our authentic selves.

Parenthood may be nothing less than trial by fire. Naturally, we can't tell one another exactly what it is like. We can,
however, share our discoveries, and we can give voice to an
ethic that maintains that children can be inherently trusted
and that life with children is inherently out of control. In
essence, while it is important to have an ethic of parenthood,
it is also important to remember that human experience is at
once ridiculous and sublime.

We seem to be living in historical times that encourage
despair, even though so much is changing for the better. The
social problems we see about us appear insurmountable,
and the solutions appear complex, if not unknown. Maybe
solutions are not that hard. Maybe we can address our social

problems from the ground up, from the beginning of human experience: the family.

Impossible medical, educational, technological, and social standards of perfection are not what families need. Families merely need room to breathe, homes, yards, and enough money to get by. Creating a brighter future can be quite simple. All we need to do is take the needs of families seriously. Take the needs of children seriously. Support families. Take care of ourselves. Take our personal needs seriously. Refuse to take ourselves seriously.

Every day in our homes we can start over. Every day we have the opportunity to begin anew. Society is no different than our homes. Every generation is a new chance to begin again. Every day with your child is a prayer of hope for the future.

From Mothering, *issue no. 72 (Summer 1994).*

when will they?

A FRIEND OF MINE, the mother of a five-month-old baby, talked recently about writing a book for parents about what babies can put in their mouths. New at going on intuition with her child, she hopes for a guidebook. Some children can put anything in their mouths and never choke; others choke easily on paper or a small piece of food; all babies will have some episodes of choking as they learn about life. A baby's impulse to put things in the mouth is totally healthy and practical. The mouth has highly developed sensors, and it is these sensors that the baby uses to give him or her information about the nature of things.

What your child puts in his or her own mouth may not be any of your business. It is your business, however, to protect your child from harm, so you will learn what objects to be vigilant about by watching your own child. This is the Parent Dance—the same dance you will dance at every transition in your child's life. It is the dance of trust in which you ask yourself if it is necessary to impact your child's own timetable. When we feel anxious about our child's behavior, we are usually really anxious about our own performance. "Am I doing enough?" "Is there anything else I need to do as a parent?" "Is there anything I can do?"

We ask ourselves questions: When will she sleep through the night? When will he let me put him down? When will she sleep in her own room? When will he use the toilet? When will they clean their rooms? When will she brush her teeth and floss? When will he be friendly again? Beneath all of our

"When will . . . ?" questions are questions of frustration or anxiety. If you sense frustration, check out whether or not you are giving too much, and do something for yourself. If you sense anxiety, be honest with yourself about what is really possible in the situation; then either take action quickly and decisively or let it go.

Children are not us. They are separate human beings. It is foolish to assume that we can control the behavior of another human being, even a baby. The budding independence of toddlers unnerves us, and well it should. It's our wake-up call, reminding us that our children do not belong to us. Our children belong to themselves.

They get to choose. We can tell them our feelings about conflicts and seek their cooperation in situations that involve us all, but we cannot control their behavior—at least not without paying a price. When we attempt to control behavior, we find ourselves when the children are older with few threats left for the really dangerous stuff. When we practice trusting our feelings, and our children's own timetables for self-regulation, we live a model of trust that makes things easier as they get older.

The Parent Dance is a three-step. One step forward, two steps back. We push children a little to see if they are "ready" or if there is something we "should do." Then we step back to see if what we've been pushing against is a habit or a need. When up against a habit, it is soft and mushy, gives a little, breaks easily into smaller pieces. Whereas a habit is elastic, a need is hard like rubber. You push against it; it pushes back. You push again; it pushes harder. A need always has to win.

In the Parent Dance, we can afford to step back because we realize that we only bear witness as parents to our child's behavior and personal development; we do not create it. In the Parent Trap, you forget that there is always someone "ahead of" or "behind" your child. There is always someone whose baby is sleeping through the night when yours hasn't a clue. Always some model teen, model student, model family, when your teen is experimenting with drugs.

The Parent Trap is really about what other people are thinking of us, how we rate on the Parent Report Card. What if our children "turn out bad" and it is our fault? That's the bottom line. Parents who cannot bear the anxiety of witnessing their children's own timetables or who resort to overpowering their children because they believe they must need reassurance for their parenting behavior and look for it in the guilt and frustration that come from comparing children to one another.

In *Daily Reflections for Highly Effective People*, author Stephen R. Covey says, "Sometimes we get social mileage out of our children's good behavior, and in our eyes, some children simply don't measure up. Our image of ourselves, and our roles as good, caring parents can be deeper than our image of our children, and perhaps, even influence it. There can be a lot more wrapped up in the way we see and handle problems than our concern for our children's welfare. It is then that, instead of trying to change them, we should try to stand apart from them—to separate us from them and sense their identity, individuality, separateness, and worth."

The truth is that you cannot "make" infants or children do anything without overpowering them. When you do that, you participate in an adversarial rather than a cooperative relationship with them. If you go for win-lose rather than win-win in your family, nobody will win. Everybody loses. Win-win, although initially more complicated, less expedient, and certainly unpredictable, promotes an ease that adversarial parenting cannot approach.

Adapting parenthood ideas from Covey's book *The 7 Habits of Highly Effective People,* we can develop ways to make nonadversarial parenting a habit.

1. *Effective parents act rather than react.* They are proactive and aware of the space between their child's actions and their own response in which they can remember who they are and remember what their vision of their child is.

2. *Effective parents remember the truth.* They keep in mind the spirit of relationship they want with their child. In all interactions with their child, they begin with this spirit.

3. *Effective parents do what they say.*

4. *Effective parents seek solutions that work for everyone.* They choose win-win rather than win-lose.

5. *Effective parents seek more to understand than to be understood.* Overcoming the impulse to judge and act, they strive to see the whole picture. They focus on the situation rather than on the character of the people involved, including themselves.

6. *Effective parents optimize situations.* Rather than seeking only to satisfy or compromise, they view conflict as an opportunity to come together for something bigger.

7. *Effective parents renew themselves.* They know that as knives and saws must be sharp to work well, so must they be well honed physically, mentally, and spiritually. They renew their relationships. They take care of themselves.

What is our job as parents? Is it to socialize our children? Although we can provide an atmosphere of love and trust and share information that may help our children become socialized, the ultimate task is theirs alone. Ultimately, it will be the peer interactions between ages 14 and 21 that will refine the socialization process. Let us think of ourselves as mentors to our children. They are our apprentices. An apprentice learns from experience. An apprentice learns by doing.

Joseph Chilton Pearce, Rudolph Steiner, and Jean Piaget would say that knowledge comes to us through conduits, through a matrix, which is the navigational center by which we interpret information. For the infant, the matrix is the mother. An infant knows discomfort, for example, yet is not psychologically mature enough to identify its cause. For that, the infant goes to the mother. The mother's ongoing and consistent interpretation of experience provides a living model for the psychological structures that will later appear in the child's psyche.

If we concern ourselves with our child's performance so that we will look good as parents, we do our child a disservice. The home is supposed to be the safe place. The world "out there" is supposed to be the bog. Our children will surely find

their critics out there; we can afford to be their allies. Allies
do not give up their individual authority, nor are they violent.
Allies have many tools for resolving conflict because they have
to. Violence and sanctions are counterproductive with friends.

You can afford to be your child's ally because ultimately it
is only love, trust, and interdependence that control behavior.
You can afford to trust yourself as a parent because you have
a track record. You can afford to trust your child because your
child is close to the evolutionary source, having been recently
imprinted by the biological imperative, as yet untouched by
society, culture, mores, race, and custom.

Yes, your baby will sleep through the night. Maybe not
when you want, maybe not until between the ages of two and
three, but for sure. Your child's sleep habits are not your fault.
That's for sure, too. Hide the clocks at night; refuse to count
hours of missed sleep. Nap when you can. Create practical
sleeping arrangements: big mattresses, lots of futons, rooms
of beds, love nests, beds under beds, and sleeping bags. Get
loose about sleep.

Your baby will "let you put him down" when he becomes
interested in other things. And believe me, this will happen
soon enough. It is the highly evolved baby who demands
holding. Holding and carrying a baby facilitate the healthy
development of the baby's neuroendocrine system. The baby
knows that to be held and to be attached is to survive. All of
the baby's behavior is directed at ensuring attachment and
survival.

Toilet training happens.

They clean their rooms when they understand money.

They brush their teeth when they start kissing.

You don't make those things happen. You're not God. All
you can do is provide deep, warm-hearted, body-and-soul
food and water, and the bumper rails to bounce off of as they
grow up. This way, you'll be giving your child the opportunity
to be an authentic human being.

Dance the Parent Dance. Forget the Parent Report
Card—you won't know your grade until the course is over
anyway. Take a breath. There is a bigger picture. There is a big-

ger dream. We don't make life happen. It happens to us, and we make choices. In giving your child self-trust by modeling trust, you give a most precious gift. Don't pretend you're God. And don't hesitate to step in for Him when you must.

From Mothering, *issue no. 73 (Winter 1994).*

the truth about nightwaking

TWENTY YEARS AGO, when I first became involved in birth and breastfeeding advocacy, I remember sitting around with a group of new mothers telling each other the truth about nightwaking. Each of us believed that ours was the only baby not sleeping through the night. We blamed ourselves. I hesitantly asked how many babies were really waking up during the night. Seventy-five percent of the moms in the room raised their hands. We all heaved a great sigh of relief. We had believed that nightwaking was an aberration.

I am sorry to say that nightwaking is still an issue that can be used to terrorize new parents. I had hoped that concern over nightwaking had gone the way of the "don't pick them up" child-torture creed of the forties and fifties. Just as we now know that picking up babies is good for them, so should we also remember that nightwaking is normal and that there is no such thing as a universal standard for sleep.

Sleep is, in fact, not a skill or a habit but an instinct and a need. It is not really something you can try to do or try to not do. It simply overcomes you. It is important to set the stage for sleep with bedtime rituals. But like talking, walking, self-discipline, and toilet training, sleep develops at the pace of the individual baby.

There are many good reasons why most babies wake regularly during the night. My son woke frequently during the night when he first began to recognize the urge to urinate and was beginning to learn to control it. Some babies move in their sleep as if they are mimicking the crawling or climbing activities of the day. Lack of fresh air and exercise can result in overtired kids.

Just as adults have trouble falling asleep or staying asleep when we are overstimulated, our babies often become overstimulated by their environment. Those children who feel, see, and hear things more acutely, who have low sensory thresholds, are often nightwakers. Nightwaking may be a sign of vulnerability to the environment. Remember that a baby's central nervous system is still maturing during infancy. The soft fontanel on the top of the baby's head reminds us that the baby is still a work in progress. With this in mind, it is obvious that sleep patterns and habits would mature according to an internal timetable. It is impossible for me to even consider that sleep, as an inherent need, would be left to regulation by human caretakers. Sleep is an instinct.

I have agonized over the nightwakings of my children. Some have been easy. Some have been hard. Some have been really hard. I have cried in my trusty rocking chair in the middle of the night and felt that I could not go on. I have kept track of missed sleep and lost hours and pitied myself throughout the day for never getting enough sleep. By the third or fourth child, however, I had learned to not look at the clock in the night, to not keep track, to not think about it when I woke up, and to try to catch up on weekends if circumstances allowed.

I was thrilled to discover that I did not have to make up sleep hour by hour. Extra hours of sleep make up for lost days of sleep. When someone has been deprived of REM sleep, he or she spends more time than usual in REM sleep and gets to that level of sleep more quickly. REM is the later stage of sleep that creative people and problem solvers particularly need. The early delta sleep that we all need for regeneration is not lost in the typical nightwaking scenario.

It is easy to blame ourselves when our baby's nighttime needs seem excessive. In fact, no aspect of parental behavior has been shown to cause nightwaking, and babies whose cries are responded to rapidly are not more prone to nightwaking. Babies who are cared for exclusively by their mothers from birth are the slowest to sleep for long stretches. The quickest to adopt adult sleep patterns are the babies who have no regular caretaker.

The current popularity of "methods" to treat sleep "disorders" is ludicrous and insulting and plays on the fears of new parents. To undermine a parent's confidence by suggesting that a natural and mostly uncontrollable instinct can be controlled in the name of discipline is to undermine the parent's confidence and to abuse the unique integrity of the child.

Children with less regular sleeping habits are not more likely to have significant emotional problems later in childhood. In fact, only 5 to 10 percent of sleep disorders in adults can be predicted by the sleeping habits of toddlers. It's actually more likely that a baby's sleep patterns are related to the length of labor, the state of the baby upon delivery, and the sleep patterns of the mother during pregnancy.

Bedtime rituals are very important. Take your time with them. Be relaxed. I still smile fondly on the oak rocker that put many a baby to sleep. Movement, whether in a rocking chair, stroller, backpack, or car, always works. Sugar, additives, caffeine, citrus, apple juice, and other foods can be overstimulating and can contribute to bedwetting, which wakes older babies. Sometimes mold in mattresses, petrochemicals, a down comforter, or a sleeping bag can be an irritant that interferes with relaxing sleep. A room too warm or too cold or clothing too confining can also contribute to restless sleep.

Current popular child development theories suggest that instead of using commonsense observations and loving tolerance, we coerce our smallest ones to follow the predictable patterns of adult sleep in order to make our own lives more convenient. Human nature, however, is more complicated than that. And while we can always force our will on others, whether they be young or old, we cannot guarantee that this submission will not lead to alienation.

Child development theorist Erik Erikson said that the crisis of the first year of life is attachment. A child learns to trust or mistrust. Trust is learned if there is adequate caretaking, warmth, touching, love, and physical care. Mistrust is learned from cold, indifferent, rejecting care. From this crisis the child

is supposed to learn faith in people and faith in the environment. The template for our future approach to new learning is
laid down in infancy.

Some other more contemporary child development
theorists advocate a mechanistic type of child rearing that is
adult-centered, adversarial, and domineering. Burton White,
in his book *The New First Three Years of Life*, advocates
"immobilizing the child for fifteen seconds" as a means of
disciplining the 8- to 14-month-old baby. For the 10-month-
old who repeatedly knocks your glasses off your face, White
recommends, "Some parents use a brief period of confinement in a playpen. Your baby will still cry, but at least you
won't have to hold him firmly. Others will withhold attention by turning away from him." White also defends Richard
Ferber, the doctor who advocates letting babies "cry it out" to
go to sleep. Gerber Products Company, in its *Little Newborn
Baby Book*, publishes the advice of psychologist C. Merle
Johnson: "Put your baby down sleepy but awake. This way,
she will learn to feel safe and comfortable in her crib and
soothe herself to sleep. While it's tempting, don't rock your
baby to sleep at bedtime. Otherwise, when she's older, your
services will still be needed when she wakes in the middle of
the night."

To suggest that we can teach or discipline an infant to sleep
in a prescribed way assumes a psychological sophistication that
the human infant simply does not possess. The human infant
does not yet engage in self-reflection and so will probably not
associate the offense with the punishment of immobilization,
confinement, or emotional withdrawal. Even if the infant can
make the association, it is questionable whether he or she will
remember it the next time the same situation occurs. And
lastly, even if the infant does remember, he or she has only
minimal self-control. It is not until age two that we can expect
to begin to discipline our children and have some reasonable
expectations of regular habits. Regulating sleep habits cannot
be called discipline. It might better be called behavior modifi-
cation, a method we usually reserve for the socially miscreant.

The truth is that most babies sleep through the night
once most of their teeth come in. Reading books, studying

"methods," attending institutes, and going to workshops will not change this, and trying to undo someone else's inherent timetable is a recipe for coercion, control, and submission. The methods designed to make the situation more convenient for the parents are not in the best interests of the child.

Each child has a unique timetable—so unique that no child before or after will ever have just this timetable again. You can mess with this timetable a bit to see what is habit, what is need. You're supposed to mess with it. But just like a rubber band, just like a pendulum, if you push too hard, if you control a child's inherent nature too much, that child will eventually rebel against you with behavior that is out of control.

Infants are not supposed to conform to our convenient, 20th-century sleep schedule, our nine-to-five lives inside houses. They are preceded by 100,000 generations of hunter-gatherers. They expect to be carried. They cannot soothe themselves. Our response to their needs creates a model for the internal psychological structures by which they will eventually be able to soothe themselves.

Babies' cries are an instinct and a resource. The reason it hurts in our bellies when we hear a baby cry is because it's supposed to. We are not supposed to be able to endure a baby's cry. It is what ensures a baby's survival. We have to take care of the baby to alleviate our own suffering.

If you have a baby who wakes during the night, know that it is perfectly normal. You can go to your baby with comfort and affection, and he or she will learn comfort and affection. If you find your baby's nightwaking terribly inconvenient, you can go to a sleep clinic where your baby will be diagnosed with a "sleep disorder" and where people who have learned about babies in institutions or through studies will give you permission to control your child's behavior so that it will no longer be inconvenient to you.

If, instead, you would consider this inconvenience part of the job description of a parent, and if you realize that this first conflict of needs sets the tone for all future conflicts with your child, then you may want to consider the corny old adage that has been passed down from generation to generation: "When they're young, they step on your toes. When they're old, they step on your heart." You can be sure they will step on your heart when they are old if you do not let them step on your toes when they are young.

From Mothering, *issue no. 76 (Fall 1995).*

finding the soul
in the city

MANY OF US FEEL A HEARTSICKNESS at the mean-spirited materialism and conformity we see reflected in modern society. Before I had children, I could pretend to distance myself from this, to "drop out" of society. Children, however, make participation in society essential, and they poignantly bring to light the disparity between the values and goals necessary to raise a healthy family and the values and goals of our society. It's a challenge to raise children who have strong personal values without making them feel like freaks or isolating them from society.

How do the values and goals of modern society differ from those necessary to raise a healthy family? Society reflects a moral relativism—anything goes; create your own reality; glorify deviation. Family life requires normalcy, common values that ensure problem solving and harmony. Modern society values things—what we have, our titles, and our possessions. Having these things gives meaning to life. This materialistic longing, however, denies the existence and importance of spirituality and disdains the metaphysical and suprapersonal. Families must value people more than things. Families must value who we are, not what we do or have. And families must believe in a deeper meaning because their experiences together demonstrate it. Modern society encourages taking and getting. Family life—moral life—requires leaving and giving.

When we speak of the cultural values that we criticize, we must ultimately admit that those values reside within all of us.

As much as we might decry the values of our culture, all we can really do to change things is to change those values within ourselves. To reconcile the paradox of living in a society of which we do not always approve, a society whose values are in transition, we must have a personal dream based on an authentic personal morality. To resist the strong message of consumerism, one must have a personal value system based on something timeless and wholly original.

We are originals as human beings, each and every one of us. If we do not want moral relativism, we must anchor our personal dream in the morality of our birthright as original human beings. As parents, we have the opportunity both to protect the inherent self-esteem of this originality in our children and to rekindle and develop it within ourselves.

But how do we protect our children's self-esteem while we're growing our own self-esteem? Is it too much work, too psychological, too impossible? No. It is truly the work of the human family. It is the work of human maturation. It is not only possible, it is necessary. With self-esteem, we can be truly resilient in any society.

Self-esteem comes from loving ourselves, having compassion for ourselves, tenderness in difficult times, and patience with and acceptance of our own distinctiveness. Self-love comes from trusting ourselves. We trust ourselves to live by our own personal values most of the time. Self-trust comes from knowing ourselves. We trust ourselves more as we get to know ourselves better.

Self-knowledge comes from spending time with ourselves. For some of us this is difficult. Some like to be alone; others have to learn how to be alone. We need a few moments every day to reflect and contemplate. Some formalize this process through meditation; others go to nature to be very quiet.

As parents of young children, it is often this time alone to reflect and gather our thoughts that we sorely miss. It's important as parents of young children that we look for opportunities for contemplative time. Nursing can be a time for contemplation if we can resist the temptation to make to-do lists in our heads. Bath time can afford a few moments for self-regeneration. Going for a walk with a babe in a backpack can be a time to think.

When we have young children, however, it is important to accept things the way they are. This is the meditation of life with small children. Young children are very demanding, but these demands are temporary and short-lived. We gain so much self-knowledge from being parents that life with children is really contemplation, a reflection in itself.

In addition to gaining self-knowledge through spending time with ourselves, we must tell ourselves the truth in order to know who we really are. We gain confidence in ourselves by confiding in ourselves. We build an inner life by keeping our own counsel and by self-observation. We can agree with ourselves. We can refuse to argue with ourselves. We can refuse to doubt ourselves. Others will do these things for us.

As we spend time with and get to know ourselves, we can begin to trust that we will not abandon ourselves emotionally. We cannot control the events of our lives, but when we trust ourselves to be on our own side, we are more resilient because we feel protected in all types of situations, and with all kinds of people.

How can we generate courage? Life gives us this courage. It provides opportunities for us to grow courage by providing situations that require courage. We always have enough to meet our difficulties.

> If when we get into a difficult situation, our will or our
> courage lessens, and we fall into the laziness of feeling
> inferior, thinking that we could not possibly accomplish
> such a difficult task, this diminishment of will cannot
> protect us from any suffering. It is important to gener-
> ate courage corresponding to the size of our difficulties.
> —Tenzin Gyatso, the 14th Dalai Lama

But how do we generate the courage to trust ourselves? We begin in self-trust by taking care of ourselves day by day. Getting enough sleep, eating well and with ceremony, making time for movement—all these assure us that we can be counted on to take care of ourselves. Otherwise, we internalize the message of our mechanistic culture by running ourselves as if we were machines. By giving ourselves time for rest and regeneration, for sharpening the saw, we treat ourselves as bigger than the culture, as generator of the culture. As ground, not figure.

To trust ourselves, we must be able to bear what we see without looking away. To do this, we have to resist overdramatizing our emotional experience or indulging ourselves in victimization and theatrics. Trust requires that we approach what we fear, say what we deny, and release what we want to control. To resist the lure of modern materialism, we must recognize illusion, delusion, and deception. And yet we must keep the dream.

Once we begin to get enough self-knowledge to recognize that we can rely upon and trust ourselves, we begin to fall in love with ourselves. When we accept ourselves most of the time, we can get back to acceptance with less and less downtime. With self-love, there is nothing to fear except our greatest potential.

The lifework of growing a personal morality from good self-esteem is accompanied by the quest for a personal dream. I believe that all personal dreams benefit from being rooted in the idea of a happy home. Our home environment can be the soul of our lives. Here we can see beauty, feel sustained, have our mood lifted. The way we create our home environment and use the space of our home will deeply affect our spirit and our ability to sustain a dream.

The ability to sustain a dream is also tended by our impulse for self-improvement. Creative and intuitive impulses are often our deepest morality.

Our morality is also reflected in the way we respond to cultural messages. We can teach our families about stereotypes, glittering generalities, and the language of persuasion. We can help our children to see the superficial by recognizing and supporting their deepest selves.

To sustain the dream, it is important to spend time with people who support the dream or who support the biggest picture of ourselves and our families. We hope for friendships with reciprocity and resiliency. We hope we will remember to ask for help.

It is important that there be white space for the dream to incubate and grow. To do this we must set realistic expectations and priorities. We can learn to say no as often as possible outside the home and yes as often as possible inside the home. We can teach ourselves to schedule birthdays, time with loved ones, and time for personal care as diligently as we do other responsibilities.

The original truth of who we are creates the history of our lives, the history of our culture. We do not improve things for our children by living a formula or by accepting the pronouncements of the critical, judgmental, or small-minded. We only improve things when we face our most possible selves and make an objective stand for original and personal freedom without license. In this, our spirit is contagious and becomes the root of the dream for our families and the foundation of a new culture.

From Mothering, *issue no. 77 (Winter 1995).*

that crazy mother

YOU KNOW HER. She's that woman over there with the unkempt look, the disheveled hair, the strident voice. She's the one who's a little too involved with her child, a little too interfering. Maybe a bit too controlling. She's that crazy mother.

What is it about becoming a parent that turns a reasonably polite, discreet woman into a guerilla warrior for her child? And why is it that no matter how righteous the cause, whenever we assert ourselves on behalf of our children, we must be prepared to do battle with the crazy mother stereotype within ourselves and in the minds of others?

With the current prominence of the Children's Defense Fund and other groups that help children, child advocacy is coming of age. Our statement of purpose in the magazine includes: "*Mothering* is a fierce advocate of the needs and rights of the child. . . ." As a magazine, we can maintain some distance from the issues of child advocacy that we cover, issues in which the child's side of the story is often not well understood or well reported. As parents, however, it takes real strength of character to be advocates for our children at times when we are either embarrassed or angered by their behavior or at a loss to understand it.

Even when we don't understand the behavior of our children, they still deserve respect and advocacy. Our well-meaning but sometimes insensitive friends may confuse us and make us feel crazy when they set standards for our children's behavior or ask repeated intimate questions about their private habits.

Sometimes we find ourselves in social situations that require impossible compliance by our children or are not appropriate for their developmental stage. At these times we may appear crazy and overprotective to others when we shield our children from experiences we judge to be questionable.

Those of us who have been led by our children into extended breastfeeding and family sleeping wonder how something that works so well can be considered crazy, and yet we feel crazy when we talk about these things to those who don't understand. Sleep deprivation, concerns for social deviation, and fear of child ruination are the stuff of the new parent's initiation. We must do our own thing with our families in order to create the definitions of a new family. We are supposed to be crazy, to be different. As young adults we do things differently than our parents. As new families we do things unique to our union. Those who are willing to be unique in a culture are sometimes looked upon as crazy.

The needs of infants and toddlers are so obvious, and they are so innocent in their demands, that we feel confident responding to them even if others question us. As our children get older, however, we may not always understand their needs quite as easily. And we sometimes have to make decisions that are unpopular with our children and may make us look crazy, even to them.

In school, a child has inevitable conflicts with friends and with teachers. In the preschool years, the issues are biting, hitting, pushing, and sharing. Everyone's child experiences both sides of these issues at one time or another. Fortunately, these behaviors are age-appropriate and not truly deviant, and they generally decline with increased capacity for language.

Parents of biters feel humiliated and confused; parents of the bitten feel violated and angry. All parents involved feel crazy, and all children involved need compassion. At times like these, the crazy parent may need to protect the child by monitoring playtimes or by rearranging play dynamics or playmates for a while. When we have children, we must sometimes bear being uncomfortable with others for the sake of our children.

School-aged children need help with friendships and with

teachers from time to time. Personality conflicts develop.
Confusing communication happens. It is a challenge for a
parent to be an advocate for a child in the classroom and not
make things more difficult for the child. Yet children must
never doubt that we will defend them. Children at this age do
not always know how to identify or what to do about unkind
or inappropriate behavior. All of us run the risk of being
labeled troublesome parents by just speaking up. Even so, it is
always worth the risk to speak up for our children, even when
we don't know whether what we do will change things at all.

Dramatic change can sometimes happen when one acts as
an advocate for a child in a medical situation. Being informed
about health care and patients' rights, understanding the
sensitivity of the emotional component of health, insisting on
reciprocity with health professionals, and being a little crazy
can all contribute to a positive outcome for children. Cancer
doctor Bernie Siegel says he can determine the health of a
patient by the nurses' notes. The ones who drive the nurses
crazy often have the strongest life force.

All parents face difficult decisions regarding infant feeding,
newborn testing, circumcision, diapers, nightwaking, sleeping, vaccinations, and so forth. Some parents also face special
medical situations that require the courage to insist on the
integrity of the child's emotional experience in the face of
necessary and sometimes lifesaving medical procedures.

Successful advocacy rests on holding a position without being positional. And while we don't always feel we can
compromise where our children's needs are concerned, we can
develop a capacity to insist on our position without insulting
others. We can be persistent. And we can have faith in the
best possible outcome, in the biggest possible picture for our
child, and for our child's capabilities.

School-aged children sometimes need their parents to
appear crazy to their friends. Young children don't always
know how to say no in social situations and may need mom
or dad to be the bad guy, to say no for them, in effect. An
alert parent sometimes has to protect an overextended child
despite protestations.

At junior high age, some parents lose track of their

children, because as children become more independent
and introspective, they appear not to need help. Quite the
contrary. This is the time when a child needs his or her worth
reflected back. Society begins to distrust this age group. Confusing issues of sexuality abound. Experimentation with hair
dye, cigarettes, and other things may tempt.

Children especially need advocates at this time and
throughout the teen years. They need advocates to others
who may judge them by their appearance and to themselves
because they may be overly self-critical. It is difficult to remain
your child's advocate when he or she is experimenting with
things of which you do not approve and which you were sure
your child would never do. It is tempting at this time to pretend that your child doesn't need you, but he or she needs you
more than ever. Things can go blurry during this time. Be an
active parent and keep faith in your child.

Even older teenagers and young adults need our advocacy.
Recently, the city of Santa Fe banned skateboarding on the city
plaza. Some adults feared being knocked down by skateboarders. The skateboarders considered themselves safe and self-
monitoring. But they had no voice. Even though they constitute a large population, teens are often discriminated against.
In matters of civil and human rights, we must be vigilant for
our kids. While they are under 18, they have no rights except
those that we impart to them. They need our protection.

We join with others when we protect our children. The
United Nations Convention on the Rights of the Child says,
among other things, that:

- All children's opinions shall be given careful consider-
  ation, and their best interests shall be protected.
- All children shall be educated in the spirit of understanding, peace, and tolerance.
- Children of minority populations shall freely enjoy their
  own culture.

Even our older children, our young adults, need special
counsel to make good choices in the transition between
childhood and adulthood. The temptations of status and materialism may lead children away from their hearts' desires.

We can help remind them of all of their capabilities, all of their needs.

In both work and education, young adults need advocacy about the bigger picture of life in the world, the fine points of their own talents, interests, and preferences, and the consequences of decisions. Our advocacy for them at this time consists of not doing too much, of tempering our generosity. Offering, not pushing. Being available, but not undermining independence or confidence. Kind of like a weaning.

Being crazy is not just for moms. Crazy dads follow in the same tradition. We're crazy any time we take an unpopular position in a group or support someone or something just because of love. We're crazy any time we stick up for our children without any evidence. I can't always control the events of my children's lives, but now and then I can get all worked up over them with such righteousness that it's awesome. At those times I realize how fierce and irrational my willingness to defend my children is, how animal-like, how instinctual. One feels in this type of attachment part of the greater good.

It's good to be a little bit crazy. A little bit crazy about your child and willing to get crazy for him or her. I'm sure there's supposed to be at least one, maybe two people who think you're the greatest no matter what. Someone who rushes to defend you without knowing the whole story. Someone who sympathizes even after knowing it. Someone who is crazy about you. The Crazy Mothers Club is open to both men and women. You can tell members by the "red badge of courage" they wear barely visible on their lapels. You can also tell them by a certain gleam in their eyes. These are the parents who are willing to get crazy for love.

From Mothering, *issue no. 78 (Spring 1996).*

before car seats

THOSE OF US WHO BEGAN PARENTHOOD in the days before car seats (early seventies) remember that wasteland of misinformation and superstition that was the legacy of the fifties. Most of us didn't know what real babies were like, and most people around us didn't talk about what real life was like. Before car seats, children were seen but not heard. The advent of car seats, as difficult as they were to become accustomed to, was also the advent of increased advocacy for children. In those days it was possible to find (white) cotton clothing for children only in secondhand stores and at JC Penney. The only natural baby products were cornstarch and almond oil.

Stylish maternity wear was nonexistent; fathers were just peeking into the delivery room; and the word *doula* was first coined by Dana Raphael, and no one knew what it meant.

And mothers, defending themselves internally from the feminist movement on the one hand and the traditional role models on the other, never gave even a thought to taking care of themselves. Postpartum care! What? Mom and Babe exercise classes? Not! Going to a movie, for a hike, out to lunch for yourself? Unheard of.

New parents today have a better idea of what family life is like because we've been talking about it more realistically for 20 years. The importance of the child is much more appreciated than was the case 20 years ago, and breastfeeding and midwifery have made good progress. A lot has changed. What hasn't changed is how hard it is to balance personal needs with family needs. What has changed is that we're trying harder to do that.

Whenever we talk about needs, I have to chuckle at this new phenomenon. Twenty years ago, we didn't know what our needs were. It took years to discover them, years more to learn to express them. And now we think we should have them met. Surprise. Knowing your needs doesn't guarantee anything, which raises the question of what we really need anyway. For babies, it's easier. Clearly they need what they want. Which is to say, even though we like to have personal time as a parent, in the early years this is sometimes rightly sacrificed to the needs of the baby or to the family as a whole.

As children get older, however, we have more opportunities to take care of ourselves, and sometimes, out of the wonderful habit of caring for others, we forget about ourselves. We have to learn to nurture and support ourselves in equal proportion to how we nurture and support others.

I find that new mothers today have more practice considering their own nurturing than we did 20 years ago. *Nurturing* is a word we didn't even use very much back then. And they have more practice integrating different personas. This perhaps gives new mothers of today a bit of a head start in handling the balancing act of early parenthood, but the real demands of family life are a surprise to us all, and we all need help with this.

As much as possible, it helps to anticipate our needs so they do not compete with other needs as much in the day-to-day chaos of family life. Regardless of birth setting, have someone who provides a safe environment with you at your birth. And make plans to be cared for by others in some way afterward. Also, ask friends to bring dinner nightly for two weeks following birth. Consider a diaper service, or ask for this as a shower or blessingway gift. Stay in your "softy" clothes after birth and spend time with your baby.

Run your home like a business. If a couple expects each other to do all the tasks necessary in a busy home, they end up having unrealistic expectations and resenting each other. Identify services that you can have done cheaply or through barter with others, such as car repairs and home improvements. Excellent natural food is available for take-out in many towns; and laundry, dry cleaning, and house cleaning services can help during busy times—or anytime.

Maybe these things seem obvious, but before car seats, new families often tried to do everything themselves. Before you have a baby, or when your children are small, identify friends you can call on for real help. Identify enough service providers, health care professionals, and educational opportunities that you have lots of choices.

As important as knowing how to pick up the pieces and knowing to get help when things are too busy is knowing how to identify when they're heading that way and pull back. The unexpected always seems to happen, and if we run ourselves at full speed, what will we do when it does? We can tell we are overwhelmed when there is no downtime, no time when nothing happens, no breaks. And when the breaks come, it's hard to relax. Or the mental track just can't shut down. It's the Frenzy and Collapse routine.

I'm beginning to see warning signs that tell me I'm heading toward Frenzy and Collapse. I may feel more tired than usual or tired when I wake up. I will become angry more easily, cry more easily, be more afraid of everything and more mentally oppressed. Now I'm beginning to see that I can head myself off at the pass if I stop and reconnoiter when I see these signs. It's just when I feel that I cannot stop that I must—reprioritize and catch my breath. If I don't, I'll end up in an emotional storm and have to stop anyway. This is the time for jammies on the floor and rethinking what really has to be done.

During times like these, or anytime, here is some first aid for a stormy soul. Sleep. I'm always amazed at what some real catch-up sleep can do. Almost everything looks better when we're not tired. And things get done so much more easily when we're focused on what we're doing and not worried about what we have to do next.

Go outside. Just getting outside with children, walking around the block or in the woods, taking a hike, or simply looking at the sky—these things bring peace. Being quiet in nature always brings clarity and rejuvenation.

Listen to music. Sometimes I need Gregorian or Hindu chants to calm a troubled soul. Other times I need rock and roll to shake out the cobwebs. Most people identify music as their number-one pleasure, and it often improves our frame of mind. Also, making music is great for the spirits. Try a drum or a rattle.

If you need to cry, go to a sad movie. If you need to lighten up, go to a funny movie. Action movies help make our troubles seem smaller and provide total escape.

Elders, in the person of the clergy, therapists, and experts who write helpful books, give perspective when we need it. Some people have to tell their story, either to friends or to professionals. Some like to write about their lives. While again, these ideas seem obvious, I have found that I lose perspective when times get out of control and that having reminders like these around helps me regain a sense of control.

It has also helped me to have on hand previously identified ideas for 15-minute relaxations that I can do at a moment's notice if I need them. This process allows a break in focus to gain perspective, reprioritize, and return with renewed creativity.

Some examples of 15-minute relaxations are having a cup of coffee or tea; watching the clouds; lying in a hammock; knitting; sitting by the window or by the fire; sitting outside; lying in the grass or on the ground; reading a poem; doing yoga, stretching, or slow dancing; just doing nothing.

I've been inspired by athletes who know how to summon their resources even in tough times, and I wonder what the attitudes are that help us in tough times. One attitude is to be able to focus outside ourselves. That's what these 15-minute relaxers do. They snap us back into reality and help us to participate in life spontaneously without undue inner focus.

Athletes have to continually start over and have the mental discipline to counteract their inner doubts and fears. Parents need this discipline—the wisdom to say, "I'll think about it tomorrow. I'm too tired now." This kindness to ourselves underscores a forgiving inner dialogue that gives us all some slack.

In the days before car seats, we didn't allow ourselves too much slack. We were coming out of the Perfect Family Ideal into the Perfectly Natural Ideal, and there were several models of perfection to choose from. And let's face it, good take-out food was just not that widely available. There were also strict food dictates for those of us who were experimenting with vegetarianism and natural foods. The Perfect Mother does not have to bake cookies or make every meal herself. She will have nearly 22,000 meals with her child. She can let a few go.

Letting go of some of our self-expectations when things bunch up can help us be better parents by being less stressed-out parents. What things are really important to do? What things do we really have to do? What can we let go? What can we postpone? What can we do next week? What will really happen if we don't do this one thing? These are questions that we always have to be asking ourselves.

And yet, like everything, let's not make an obsession out of getting our needs met. If we're lucky, we will. If we try hard, we might. But we often have to let everything go for the new needs of the moment. It's an ongoing dilemma, and we get better at it. It helps when we have the inner honesty to fairly witness our own lives. It helps if we tell ourselves the truth about what we see. It makes a difference if we neither deflate nor inflate ourselves.

Both before and after car seats, it has been hard to keep the balance between self and others. Being a parent makes it quite a challenge. As a parent of teens and young adults, I look back on the time when I didn't know my own needs, didn't make time for myself. And you know what? It wasn't so bad. Looking back, I remember that part, but now I remember the part I took for granted then. The baby. At the time, I felt oppressed by the needs of others. Now I know that I was in the presence of God.

From Mothering, *issue no. 80 (Fall 1996).*

the wonder of children

Nora and I were having dinner at a local cafeteria before going to the movies last Friday night. While in line, we saw a loving family whom we noticed several times that evening. The parents were obviously crazy about each other. The baby was dressed all in pink, with pink elastic lace around her ankles and pink bows in her hair. Her patent leather shoes were bright red. The parents were patient with the baby, and her older brother loved to walk around with her in the cafeteria.

As I observed how comfortable this family was with one another in public and how at ease the entire establishment and its patrons were with children, I was grateful that we as a society are comfortable with children in public places. Children help civilize us.

In our fast-paced civilization, we are accustomed to instant gratification, and that can give rise to unrealistic goals for ourselves and our children. The accomplishments of our children or the idealization of our own lifestyle can become the measures by which we value ourselves. In a materialistic society we are forever getting somewhere. Children remind us that we are always already there.

We hear so much bad news from the media, and as a society, we emphasize the problematic and sensational. We define our experiences in stress levels, and we often feel overwhelmed. New parents have a right to be overwhelmed. They are in the grip of the unpredictable and the uncontrollable. Yet I am grateful that children are so unpredictable, so uncontrollable. They remind us of both our fallibility and our preciousness.

To keep perspective, I remember what I am grateful for, what is right with things—the things so obvious and so poignant about living with children that in taking them for granted, we underestimate our lives. When we see life in a positive light, we have things to look forward to and are grateful for what we have. Looking forward and feeling grateful help in difficult times and are customary in good times.

I read yesterday that 25 percent of the families in my state are hungry; the state I live in is second only to Mississippi in numbers of families living in poverty. I'm not hungry. I'm hardly ever cold. I have good health, loved ones, interesting work. The rest is extra. The time we spend complaining about the bad things could be spent transforming them.

My children have been and continually are a delight to me. Being with them and participating in their world, the world of the moment, the world of sensation, I am ever renewed with wonder. Their newness makes everything possible. Their freshness is miraculous.

Every day the earth is bombarded by cosmic dust; every moment it is new. Ninety-eight percent of the atoms in our bodies are replaced each year. Our bodies change biochemically as our thoughts change. Babies are the continual renewal and rebirth of life.

Like many parents, I feared the teen years but found them to be another time of renewal and rebirth. One of my biggest surprises has been the gift of humor that my children have given me from these years. With three in their teens and several friends in and out of the house, I was vastly outnumbered. I found humor to be a way of saying hard things, of being honest while still protecting fragile self-images. Humor is respectful. Humor is the way teens speak to one another. Teens use words to play with each other. It's fascinating how they reinvent the language with their creativity. Many of the words we enjoy began as teen slang words. "Dude!"

My children continually invite me into the physical world. Their physical natures and their enthusiasm for the outdoors open me to test my physical limits. I am more brave with them, and because they tolerate my fears, I try new things with them. We can forget as parents that while we are always imparting knowledge to our children, they have a body of knowledge to impart to us too.

I have learned a new way to approach mechanical devices from my children. My oldest daughter taught me not to panic when approaching something that was broken. I now observe it, analyze it, and often fix it. My sons have taught me that fear of physical challenges and risks can be exhilarating (I'm still working on that), and their patience with my fears helps me take them less seriously.

I wonder if I would have gone as many places or traveled as far if not for my children. I have always wanted them to see new places, and for years I searched for the perfect beach. I never would have gone to some of those spots or planned the trips I did without the excitement of sharing them with the kids.

I'll never forget the time we were in Mexico. I was crazy to have taken them all down there. We were in a restaurant where we were attempting to speak Spanish. The restaurant was next door to a church. Just after we ordered, the choir in the church started singing as the dogs in the street started howling, and we were sure we were in a werewolf movie.

That was the trip on which they got me to agree to a ride on a banana boat that bounced about the bay while I feared for their lives. We've learned to negotiate busy city traffic and many airports, and they really know how to pack. They've forced me to pack lighter because they won't haul my overload anymore. I've learned to kayak, canoe, sail, and snorkel (not unattended) because I wanted my kids to learn how. We've all learned from expanding our horizons and from being with each other in new surroundings.

Because we've gone new places, we've come to enjoy trying new food. And I have been more adventurous with my cooking as they have gotten older. The willing, hungry, and always complimentary audience of my children and their friends for Sunday dinner has allowed me the creative freedom to experiment and develop new dishes.

This creative freedom was possible because of their patience and appreciation, a patience and appreciation they learned from my tolerance of their individual and childish timetables. In the early years with children, things are so free-form that it is an enormous opportunity to learn patience and respect for personal style. And we can also develop compassion as we appreciate the limitations they face, even when they are trying their best. From the tenderness and tolerance we show our children, we grow to be softer with ourselves.

We can also learn to focus in the midst of interruptions. When we live organically with children, incorporating them into our activities and working with them present, we learn to regain our focus even with interruptions, to pay attention to several things at the same time, and not to lose track of important details. Children are a great training ground for the high-level executive.

Holding, rocking, and feeding a baby are all intimate activities. This intimacy is so powerful that it opens hearts. After my first child was born, I remember being surprised that I was so moved by news of sad circumstances that I would cry if I read the newspaper or heard of tragedy. Call it postpartum hormones if you will, but I know that my sensitivity heightened after I gave birth.

Because life with children is so poignant and my love for them so deep and pervasive, being a parent forces me to make peace with death. At first it seems impossible to speak rationally of death once one has the attachment of children. Death is inconceivable. However, it is only the acceptance of the inevitability and unpredictability of death that makes it possible to live life in the moment, the way children do.

I have so much to be grateful for as a parent. Not only have my children given me a rebirth of wonder, a look at the world through new eyes, a sense of humor, an appreciation and comfort level with the physical world, a playful look at language, travel opportunities, eating adventures, compassion, patience, focus, and a spiritual dialogue, they have given me myself. The more I've been myself with my children, the more I've been myself with others. They are so real; they make it easy for me to be real.

I've had the opportunity to raise my children pretty much as I'd hoped and in keeping with my values. Of course, plenty of unexpected events have occurred along the way, and we have had easy and hard times, like everyone. But we are lucky. We continue to like each other and to enjoy one another's company. And we all have a lot to look forward to.

When I was the parent of young children, I thought things sort of ended when they were 18; now I know that couldn't be further from the truth. I'm looking forward to the way I will change when I revisit my young adult years as my children begin theirs.

I'm grateful for the friendship and companionship of my children as they get older, and I look forward to reinventing family with them at this stage of life. Even knowing the risks and uncertainties of the world, I want to say yes every day to life. My children help me do that. How do we remember the wonder that children bring to our lives in the daily juggling of our worries and burdens? Children necessarily lean on us, and often we just have to carry on. Life with them is demanding. It is exhausting. It requires constant creativity and attention. And it gives back so much.

If we look at things from the materialistic point of view, we may believe that children slow us down; that they hinder us. From what? It is their childish natures that renew daily life, and they renew us. The authentic world of the child provides opportunities for us to both participate in their timeless reality when we are able and to transform emotions and perceptions when we are not. Ongoing transformation is in keeping with the patterns of nature and, thus, is imperative for our maturation.

From Mothering, *issue no. 82 (Spring 1997).*

rave on

RECENTLY, I HAPPENED UPON a national television evening news and commentary feature program about raves. The coverage centered on the unfortunate deaths of several young people who had had lethal reactions to drugs acquired at raves. The coverage concluded that raves were dangerous and failed to point out any redeeming factors associated with them. Even the teens interviewed on the program did not articulate their popularity well.

It struck me immediately that this was another one-sided look at the lives of teens and young adults. Of necessity, they act out the dark side of society and are blamed for it when they do. The experiences that the teens I know have had with raves have been positive, and I understand them in quite another way.

A rave is a chaotic music and dance event. It originated in Great Britain when members of a rock and roll band noticed the transcendent, timeless state they sometimes experienced when the music, the crowd, and the moment all felt in harmony. They tried to replicate this harmony through performances where liquor and cigarettes were not present and where the music had a strong rhythm.

Raves today are a combination of music, dance, and technology. By manipulating two turntables, a DJ plays a combination of unique music, made on the spot to accompany the rhythms of the group. Independent record labels also produce techno, house, trance, ambient, and other music for raves. People dance to the music accompanied by strobe lights and video images projected on the walls. Sometimes there is music

of different tempos in different rooms—cooling down music
in one room, for example

Raves follow in the tradition of trance music and dance.
All indigenous cultures have traditions for invoking the trance
state through drumming, dancing, rhythmic repetition, sleep
deprivation, and sometimes psychoactive substances. The
purpose of the trance in traditional cultures is to experience
the transcendence and timelessness the British musicians who
first started postmodern raves described.

While caution regarding drug use for teenagers and young
adults is warranted, let's not make the mistake of dismissing
what may be an actual spiritual experience for some participants because it is also sometimes the scene of drug experimentation and transgressions.

It is normal for teens and young adults to experiment
with sex, alcohol, and drugs. What is of concern is abuse,
when experimentation becomes habit and interferes with life.
Because drugs are illegal, young people can come in contact
with criminals, and their innocence can be exploited by those
who make dangerous mixtures of drugs. But this contact and
exploitation can occur at any gathering where large numbers
of teens hang out, not only at raves. How can we protect our
teens from exploitation at raves and other communal settings
without taking their special gathering place away?

This "special gathering place" is the creation of the young
and the artistic. We are generally dismissive of the lives of the
young except when they bother us. Because of this we may not
see that teens are starving for the sacred and that it is with this
hunger that they go to raves.

You may be surprised, as I was, to know that raves are
infusing new enthusiasm into traditional religious worship.
For the last eight years or so, the Nine O'clock Service (NOS),
a young Anglican congregation from Sheffield, England, has
been refining its rave-style "Planetary Mass." The NOS community was founded in the mid-eighties by musicians and
multimedia artists.

Scripture from numerous liturgical traditions is read at
every mass, and the words are set against a pulsating audio
backdrop of techno music and visual images that cover

screens around the room and convey spiritual as well as envi-ronmental messages.

The NOS Planetary Mass has received the endorsement of Sheffield's Anglican bishop, the Rt. Reverend David Lunn, who views it as "reinfusing a struggling church with a sense of the sacred." It has also been supported by the Rt. Reverend William Swing, the Episcopal bishop of California. In 1994 the first Planetary Mass was held at San Francisco's Grace Cathedral.

The Planetary Mass is an hour of sacred ritual. Images of spiraling galaxies are projected on walls. Television moni-tors play images of nature and the environment. Contagious techno ambient music invites participants to dance and be part of a community experience of joy and transformation.

Matthew Fox, the theologian who has been writing about ecstatic worship for many years, believes that the Planetary Mass has all the elements of ritual renewal. It has a sense of order and meaning. It is physical, playful, participatory, uncontrolled, and prophetic.

The parallels between the experiences our young people seek through the rave and what people of all ages seek from a spiritual experience are clear. Let's not fail to see the depth and true nature of our young people's lives because of our own prejudice.

Too much in society is prejudicial to teens and young adults. I read recently of renewed attempts to create dress codes for public schools on the pretense that they improved grades and discipline. The offending clothing was baggy pants. It was suggested that baggy pants might even lower one's grade point average.

Now I realize that the current fashion for teen males is the hoodlum look, but is it really any more offensive than the rolled up sleeves with cigarettes of the fifties or the bell-bottom jeans with patches and fringe of the sixties? Fashion is always a statement and one of the few avenues of originality that young people have.

In our town, skateboarders and Hacky Sackers have been banned from the plaza because, as it has gotten busier, these activities have been perceived as dangerous by those unaccustomed to them. While a nearby skateboarding area has been created, it still remains clear that the ban was an act of prejudice against young people, who have no vote and little voice in matters that affect them.

When I was growing up on military bases, there were always teen clubs. These were simple areas with a couple of rooms, comfortable chairs or booths, Ping-Pong tables, pool tables, and a jukebox or DJ music. We paid minimal dues or an entrance fee. Even in this very conservative atmosphere, this was a place where something was happening, where things were getting stirred up. We have a teen center in our town, but it is rare for communities today to provide meeting places for teens. A stronger argument could be made against raves if teens had anywhere else at all to go.

The ecstatic tradition has a strong spiritual and religious history: in shamanic and Vedic traditions, in Buddhism and Christianity. It exists in art, in transcendental poetry, in the 13th-century Sufi poetry of Rumi and others—in much that we are fascinated with now.

The ecstatic tradition explains the popularity of raves. Young people are hungry for experiences of ritual and community. I bring up the parallel between raves and religious renewal not to endorse them but to give credibility to teen experience. As participants in raves, teens are once again on the cutting edge of society. They are heralding coming trends, even starting them. In making sense of society for themselves, they reinvent it for us.

Even though young people reinvent society, we patronize them. The news coverage of raves I watched never provided a reasonable explanation for the rave phenomenon, and the reporters did not even bother to look for one. The coverage thus implied that teens were so stupid that they would participate in something en masse all over the world because it was meaningless except as a place to get drugs.

We have got to stop treating our teens and young adults as if they are second-class citizens, as if they are stupid. We call it "drug education" when we say, "Just say no to drugs," and yet we give teens little information on which to base their decision making if drugs are offered to them or on how to differentiate between drugs if they do choose to experiment. We broadcast television in which every other ad is for an over-the-counter drug and publish magazines that routinely advertise prescription drugs, and we wonder why our message of "Just say no" isn't enough.

The Consumers Union report *Licit and Illicit Drugs* and the more recent book *Marijuana Myths, Marijuana Facts* by sociologist Lynn Zimmer and physician and pharmacologist John P. Morgan offer detailed analyses of drug research and yet are seldom made available to teens and young adults. Instead, drug education assumes abstinence and does not educate for responsible drug use or occasional experimentation in a culture in which alcohol, tobacco, and caffeine are consumed routinely and in which marijuana, the fourth most popular psychoactive drug in the world, is tried by half of those between the ages of 18 and 35.

It seems reasonable with this kind of statistic to distinguish between drug use and drug abuse in our drug education. This is one way we can help prevent the tragedies of lethal drug reactions, reactions that cannot be averted by black and white information about drugs or by prohibitions.

In the dictionary, the definition for *rave* has words like *irrationality, delirium, wildly, extreme enthusiasm, violently, madness,* and *frenzy* associated with it. Many of these words can also refer to teens themselves during those years of tumultuous growth. During the early teen years, they undergo bigger changes than at any other time in their lives. We attempt to contain this tremendous upheaval with our dress codes and curfews, but what we risk containing also is the wild enthusiasm that is an open channel for the sacred.

Teens are the scapegoats and prophets of society. We scapegoat them when they show us what we don't want to see. When they show us how ridiculous our obsession with size is by purposely wearing clothes several sizes too big, we think they are stupid. When they dance all night long to a rhythmic overload in order to feel high, they remind us of the quality of prayer and transform worship.

With underpinnings in authentic drug education, I support raves and the ideas of community, celebration, and spirituality that they embody. If youths are corrupted by the greedy, it is not because they are inherently flawed but because the greedy always try to take advantage of the innocent. I say to the youth of today, "Rave on." Rave on with your wild enthusiasm, your crazy schemes, your basic out-of-control. Even though I sometimes find you irritating, confusing, and inconvenient, I realize that your excesses clean out the spark plugs of the old ways.

Rave on.

From Mothering, *issue no. 83 (Summer 1997).*

in their hands

WHEN OUR CHILDREN ARE YOUNG, we hold their lives in our hands. This is a serious charge. It changes us. As our children grow older, however, we begin to put ourselves in their hands. And when we do, we are glad that the history we share is so deep.

Recently, I took a road trip with three of my kids to visit my son, who was a whitewater river-rafting guide for the summer. I knew as soon as my son told me he was going to be a guide that I would have to go on the river and face my fear of the rapids.

It was not the first time that parenthood has pushed me to go beyond a limited sense of myself. I've previously put myself in my children's hands for other adventures. I believe my son if he tells me, "It's all good, Mom." I know that I am truly accommodated, that my weakness is tolerated, and that my fears are responded to with good humor.

My son, on the other hand, is friends with fear. He likes to snowboard fast down frozen water in the winter and raft down fast-moving water in the summer. As a one year old, he would lie with his ear to the floor and listen to the water as it rushed down the drain beneath the toilet. As he listened, he said his first word, *chine!*—short for "machine." His first love was a lawn mower. He walked at about the same age and never minded falling. This was also the baby who spent the first six months of his life either in arms or in a red Snugli baby carrier. He was very dependent before he became very independent.

This was a baby who liked contact, who demanded contact,

who wanted always to be in touch, who in every way is a very physical person. We are often impatient with babies because they are so physical. The popular media suggest that we have to train our babies to control themselves, to be independent, to sleep, and to obey, as if these were not things that had intrinsic values and would be learned naturally, as a matter of course, in human society.

How dangerous for our society that we distrust the very behavior that is the most necessary for human survival. It is those babies who demand to be attached who are the most evolved. And it is the most securely attached babies who will have the best chance of being the most resilient adults. Resiliency comes from having internalized the functions of an empathic mother and father.

There is an inherent order in the nature of things, despite the protests of those who suggest that babies must be taught basic human instincts and made compliant for the convenience of adults. Nature never contradicts itself, and we can look to nature when we are confused about how to respond to our children or about making difficult decisions.

Parents are faced with a myriad of decisions, as we are often torn between the advice of the experts and our own inner voices. We sometimes think there must be an answer outside of ourselves, that we can counter the anxiety of being totally responsible for another human being by comforting ourselves with some "dependable" solution. And while there are tried-and-true solutions that parents have shared with each other from time immemorial, it is really much simpler than that.

Today, or in any age, there is really only one decision that underlies all other decisions concerning our children. This decision is whether we will choose love or fear; whether we will choose to cooperate or to be adversarial with our children; and whether we will see them as our equals or wield authority over them. These are the qualities that form the underpinnings of our parenting decisions and the underpinnings of all actions we take.

Sometimes, when worried about our own self-image, we react with inappropriate fear and authority. At other times, we choose fear and authority because of legitimate concerns over immoral, illegal, or unsafe behavior. How we make our parenting decisions underscores what we believe about human beings, about human nature, about the nature of the child. Are order and purpose inherent in our child's development, or must we as parents bring this order and purpose to our child's life?

It's funny, in a way, that we have so much trouble trusting our loved ones. Every day we walk into rooms and buildings built by strangers we'll never see, and we don't give a second thought to their inherent integrity. We drive on highways with strangers, highways built by other strangers, and daily we entrust our lives to them all. Children are an easy excuse to indulge in fear.

Our bodies have autonomic nervous systems whose functions are automatic. They are not voluntary. This means that for the really important things, nature has hardwired a system that cannot be disrupted except under extraordinary circumstances. We cannot stop our breathing no matter how hard we try without extraordinary devices. If we hold our breath, we will simply pass out. We cannot will our heart to stop, nor can we touch or hurt our heart without extraordinary means. Nature never leaves the really important things to chance. What is the source of our breathing and our heart rate? It's a mystery that we trust every moment.

The English word *trust* comes from the Scandinavian word for "faithful"—full of faith. To trust ourselves is to be true to ourselves. Faith is in itself a leap. Our faith is not based on evidence but exists regardless of the evidence. Faith is not a conclusion but an affirmation. We can have faith in ourselves as parents, in our unique challenges and decisions, because we have faith in our children as accurate barometers of the biological imperative.

Our children are born hardwired for survival. Their needs and wants are the same. They know what they need, and they demand it. In hunter-gatherer societies, being in the arms of the mother meant that the infant was safe from the tiger. In modern times, being held in another's arms still means survival. The single most important factor responsible for an infant's normal mental and social development is *physical holding and carrying*. Infants *need* to be in arms. They know it, and they let us know it.

Current fashions and customs conspire against these natural and necessary needs of human infants. Devices such as the plastic infant carrying tray, pacifiers, cribs, and bottles are ways to distance ourselves from our babies, to gain a respite from the intimacy they require for full human development. Trends in perceiving the life of the home as servitude and drudgery, as well as lack of economic support for the family, also conspire to separate us from our loved ones, as these trends quite literally put physical distance between us.

Human infants don't like physical distance. They like constant physical contact. They expect it. They need it. And they're totally content when they have it. But how do we learn to surrender to this fierce need when others warn us that we must teach our infants to sleep, to be independent—and certainly not spoil them?

It's ridiculous to think that nature would leave a function as important as sleep to foolish parents, some of whom would look at each other on their child's eighth birthday and exclaim, "Oh, honey, we forgot to teach little Cindy how to sleep!" Sleep is a need, not a habit. It's an instinct. It takes care of itself because in nature all essential functions take care of themselves.

Holding and carrying infants also take care of themselves because nature gives babies such endearing qualities that they are irresistible. Responding to their inherent needs develops qualities necessary for our survival as adults, qualities such as consciousness, patience, generosity, kindness, and bravery. In Darwin's original writings, *survival of the fittest* refers to those individuals and societies who are the most sympathetic. A sympathetic culture has the attributes necessary for survival. Nature itself is sympathetic.

Infants don't like to be held only during the day; they like to be close at night, too. That's human nature. Yet we treat our infants worse than we treat any other humans or even animals. Under no circumstances would we leave a crying adult, friend or stranger, alone in a room without extending our condolences and offers of help. We pride ourselves on this kind of civility. We sleep with our pets. New puppies and kitties get to come into the bedroom if they cry.

Just as it is perfectly natural for animals to sleep together in groups, it is perfectly natural for human infants to want to sleep with their parents. All animal babies sleep with their mothers. Over time, human infants teach theirs parents to enjoy touch again.

Our infants are hardwired to bring their discomfort to their parents. Crying is their language. The parent is their interpreter. The infant's sense of discomfort is nonspecific and undefined. As they mature, they learn to differentiate sensations and associate them with certain experiences, so that in time they can specify and name their discomfort. This takes months, even years. Nowhere in the animal kingdom do we see intolerance of the dependency of infancy. In all of nature, dependency is protected and indulged.

It is obvious that dependency is feared by many adults. Many are hungry for intimacy but afraid to surrender. Yet life with infants *is* a surrender. When we just give up and give them what they need, it becomes so easy. It reminds me of the true meaning of the Sabbath—a day of leaving things just as they are, not trying to change them, and not *doing* anything. With infants, we are but humble servants to what *is*.

This kind of surrender has three enemies. They are fear, denial, and control. Whenever we have trouble trusting our infants, we are usually in the grip of one of these visitors. They always accompany actions of deep consequence. They are the guardians who hone our self-esteem. For it is the difficulties of being a parent that forge us into fuller human beings, with the track records and courage to face new difficulties. These new difficulties are better faced when we tell ourselves the truth and see things unclouded by fear, denial, and control.

What you fear, approach. What you deny, say. What you control, release. With fear, denial, and control aside, you can see things in your own unique and authentic way.

It is our very innocence as parents, our freshness and inexperience, that redeems us. With each new family, nature has another chance. Another chance for happy accidents that can change the course of history. Another chance for amateurs to do something no one else has ever done before. Another chance for genius.

Don't listen to the experts. Forget about them unless they come over and help you put your baby to sleep. Forget about them unless they'll remember your baby's name in 20 years. Don't give up your authority as a parent to people who don't know your baby as well as you do *or who don't know your baby at all.*

Don't stand unmoving outside the door of a crying baby whose only desire is to touch you. Go to your baby. Go to your baby a million times. Demonstrate to your baby that people can be trusted, that the environment can be trusted, that we live in a benign universe. The crisis of the first year of life is whether to trust or mistrust. Which will your baby learn?

Someday you'll need your grown-up baby to come to you. Someday you'll be in the hands of your baby. Will your baby protect you in the rapids, or will he be intolerant of your fears and weaknesses, of your dependencies?

The way you give to your baby now is the beginning of all that.

From Mothering, *issue no. 85 (Winter 1997).*

the tenderness of boys

MY SONS AND THEIR FRIENDS have been at home this weekend, and the house as been full of the sweetness of boys. Hanging around with them watching videos of their whitewater river-rafting adventures, and hearing tales of four-wheel woes, I am so poignantly reminded of how tender boys are.

For the last several decades, we've been focused on the inequality between men and women in the marketplace, and we've made progress in closing the gender gap. Women now have much greater access in society, and we have matured in our tendency to objectify, stereotype, and harass women.

However, we have not even begun to look at how we objectify and stereotype men. Many men themselves believe the lie, the lie that men are inherently flawed. For example, most of us are all to willing to believe that there are legions of shiftless single dads out there who don't pay child support because they just don't care. In fact, most fathers who fail to pay child support do so because they don't have access to their children.

The Million Man March on Washington was a great show for the strength of men. However, its underlying premise was patronizing to men and was based on the assumption that men are flawed. We expect women to be good mothers and are surprised when they are not. We hope that men will be good fathers and are surprised when they are. Why can't we simply expect men to be good fathers? This is no less than they expect of themselves.

It is difficult to keep expectations high in the face of the challenges that some families face. Poverty is one of the worst challenges. Public policy can be discouraging when it is based on the worst assumptions about fathers—as if some men, some families, are just not salvageable. Where is our hope in restoration, in renewal, in change? Where is our hope?

We are too eager to find fault with men, and the belief that some men are just not salvageable starts in the beginning, in the way we treat men as boys. Often the very characteristics that are unique among boys are not well tolerated in the orderly family or the structured school. A high proportion of boys are kinesthetic learners, people who learn best when movement accompanies learning. Many adults are impatient with these types of learners.

Recently, I saw a woman with her two sons in a beauty shop on a lazy Saturday afternoon. It was early fall and raining for the first time in months. Her eight-year-old son went outside to play, and as he left she repeatedly admonished him not to play in the water. Well, naturally he was going outside to play in the water. When he returned, she proceeded to scold him for getting his shoes wet as she remarked to me, "Oh, boys!" with disgust, as though I would know exactly what she meant. I wish I had replied, "Oh, mothers of boys!" How quickly we teach them to disdain their natural impulses.

A five-year-old boy I know was teased recently at kindergarten for wearing nail polish. He's very hip and masculine, as is his grown-up brother, who preferred pantyhose with his football helmet as a toddler. I'm quite sure sexual preference is not determined by nail polish or pantyhose, at least not before puberty.

Cosmopolitan magazine recently had a quiz in which men who dressed nicely, liked to buy furniture, and cooked were considered questionable. Stephen Harris, former editor of *Full-Time Dads,* laments the lack of support for dads at home, who are often stereotyped as less than masculine, lazy, and inept.

We traditionally hold men to very fixed behaviors and therefore risk reactive behaviors that develop from such repression. Men have much less latitude in areas of dress, occupations, and relationships than do most women in modern society. We've seen a lot of "coming out" in film and television lately, but

almost entirely about gay women. For the love of gay men to
have credibility, it is almost always presented in the context of
AIDS, even though gay men with AIDS represent a very small
percentage of the male gay population.

I bring this up because our tolerance level for gay men
speaks to our tolerance level for men in general. I was at a
workshop this summer where I observed two men my age
with their arms around each other's shoulders and their legs
touching. I assumed they were lovers only to find out later
that they were old friends recently reunited. I realized that if
they had been women, I would not have assumed that they
were gay so quickly.

Boys are demeaned in other ways. A lot more boys than
girls are diagnosed with ADD. If there were a condition, disorder, or disability with an equally high percentage of girls, it
would be studied with grant money, and gender bias would
be suggested. When a high percentage of boys have ADD, we
find it easier to accept because we already suspect that boys
my be inherently aggressive or out of control.

More men are in prison; more men commit violent crime.
More men are depressed. Men have higher rates of illness and
die sooner than women. It is men who are really the more
fragile of the sexes.

It seems odd for me as a woman to be speaking for the
vulnerability of men, but as the mother of two boys and two
girls, I have seen no difference in emotionality or expressive-
ness between girls and boys as children. So I believe that when
these things are valued in the family, even when they are not
fully valued in society, we can raise boys who are comfortable with the emotional just as we hope to raise girls who are
comfortable with the physical. As the mother of men, I am
interested in how to protect the tenderness of boys, how to
raise sons who don't forget how to cry.

In the 1960s, we focused on the ways that men and women
are the same because we were learning to be more equal with
one another. However, we also need to remember to differentiate, not only between the sexes but among individuals. Boys
are subject to social prejudices just as girls are. Although the
prejudices toward boys are more socially acceptable, they are

no less limiting. If we're going to lament the underdeveloped math and science intelligences of junior high girls, let's also lament the underdeveloped emotional intelligence of junior high boys.

No wonder men die sooner, have more illness, and explode into violence. One is enraged to the extent that one is abused by others, either emotionally, psychologically, or physically. We lose too many men to the behaviors of violence, behaviors that have their origins in the repression and violence of childhood. More physical punishment and child abuse is directed at boys and tolerated among boys, and thus boys grow up to be more violent than girls.

The rage of men, whether it turns into domestic violence, child abuse, drug addiction, or crime, is a problem for all of us. It's wrong to think that boys are tough and "can take it" or will be made tough by cruelty. People, whether male or female, are only made cruel by cruelty.

Boys and men are at more risk than we realize. The rather strict definitions of manly behavior in the US today can put undue pressure on some boys and men. How can we raise sons who retain the tenderness and emotional intelligence that young boys have? At the same time we're raising girls who can be astronauts, let's raise boys who can be stay-at-home dads.

So what can we do as parents? We can be careful about the language we use, careful about passing our own stereotypes to our children. We can forgo making statements that begin with phrases like "Girls don't. . ." or "Boys always. . ."

We can avoid making gender-prescriptive statements to our children and explain when others make them. For example, don't tell your kinesthetic, wrestling five-year-old boy to go easy on the girls. But do tell him to go easy on anyone less skilled than he is, and teach him how to wrestle without using all his strength by wrestling with him without using all your strength.

The big debate in the 1970s and 1980s was about dolls and trucks—dolls for the boys, trucks for the girls. We thought that would do it. But of course it's not that simple. Some girls just want dolls; some boys just want trucks—and there's a lot in between. So certainly, it's good to provide lots of different toys for all children and not to make any assumptions about what they like until they show you. Also, be aware of how your own suggestions can color your child's preferences.

Provide dolls and trucks, trucks and dolls, toys of all kinds for your kids—the more toy options, the better. These don't have to be store-bought toys. They can be recycled toys, homemade toys, whatever. Plus your kids will get toys from relatives and friends who have different ideas than yours. But kids are resilient. Few toys can really hurt them. Just keep striving for diversity and have the patience to let them grow out of things.

It seems to me that play choices have a lot to do with what's in the environment. I watched as the play of my children evolved from the oldest to the youngest. My oldest daughter influenced her younger brothers to play costume dramas and dolls. My boys influenced their younger sister to play "guys" and GI Joes. It's hard to say what was what, what influence prevailed because someone was a girl or boy. It always seemed to me to have more to do with who they were as people. They chose play as children that now makes perfect sense to me as I see them becoming adults.

Try not to limit behavior or activity based on gender but rather on capabilities and interests. It seems important to explain how society sees things when discrepancies come up. If there are differences, give your child tools for integration, for accepting differences between people, whether they are over gender bias, religion, or point of view. If we want boys to keep their tenderness, we must be tender mothers and tender fathers. We must demonstrate tenderness to ourselves and to others, and we must refrain from using physical force to teach or discipline.

On Friday, I spoke with a woman whose three-year-old was a bundle of energy, and the woman was being chastised by her sister for not being able to control her son. I assured her that all this was normal, both her son and her sister, and that in time he would be better able to handle social situations.

On Sunday, I watched a video of my 22-year-old son and his friends rafting and kayaking in whitewater rapids. The fearlessness that was required for them to do their daring deeds was the same fearlessness that pours out of a three-year-old. It's highly ironic to me that qualities we decry in the three-year-old—the intense focus and ability to flow with a situation—are what save the life of a 20-year-old.

I think we need to lighten up on boys, stop scapegoating men for all the ills of society (was it not women who stood by when men went to war?), and let things take their course. We don't need to protect children from a wrong turn in gender. We can trust that they will develop in their own individual and natural way within the family and normal society.

Don't forget to hug boys. Be with them when they cry without demeaning them. Encourage their deep strengths, their staying power, their loyalties. Keep the well of their tenderness open for them as they try on the mantle of society. Trust their independence and don't cling to them. Be the place they come home to when they want to soften. It is from the soft place that the deep strength comes.

From Mothering, *issue no. 86 (January–February 1998).*

children who kill

RECENT SHOOTING SPREES AND MURDERS of schoolchildren shock us. We weep for the victims and are incredulous of the assailants. We simply cannot understand the out-of-control, premeditated behavior of violent children.

Some want to blame the schools, but institutions follow legal policies enacted by the citizenry and cannot be held responsible for psychopathic or sociopathic behavior. These behaviors have their roots in infancy. Some call these children predators, some want to prosecute them as adults, execute them, and learn nothing from them.

A connection exists between these acts of violence in youth and the experiences of infancy. Early experiences affect later behavior in enduring ways. Those who work with psychopathic killers see a correlation between psychopathic behavior in adulthood and extreme multiple separations from caregivers in the early years. It will probably come to pass that the young murderer in Oregon has some attachment disorder, has been the victim of abuse, and is without conscience because of early experiences.

How does conscience develop? It is the by-product of a healthy attachment process in infancy. If we attach securely to one consistent caregiver in the first three years of life, we develop affection and this mediates our self-interest. If we do not attach securely, we may not know affection or how to mediate our self-interest. At best we are dependent on the other for our self-worth; at worst we are without conscience and feel emotions only in extreme instances.

What else do we know about violence? We know that we use more guns than other countries and that we are exposed to a lot of violence through television and other media. Have these guns and these superficial television shows made us a violent society? No. These things are the products of our violence; they did not create it. Where does this violence originate?

Human beings are not violent by nature. *The Origin of the Species* tells us that those societies most likely to survive are those that are the most sympathetic. Likewise, when anthropologists study indigenous people all over the world, they see a correlation between violence in adulthood and lack of touch in infancy. Anthropologist Margaret Mead observed one particularly violent tribe that hung their babies in hammocks and seldom touched them.

In our society, we debate about how much to touch our infants. Should we go to them in the night? Should we let them cry it out? With all due respect, these kinds of decisions are the origins of violence. Any attempt to exercise power over another can be an act of violence. Our ambivalence about touch, about dependency, about physical affection, about the body is the underpinning of a violent society.

Holding and touching our infants and children is perhaps the *most important thing* we can do to ensure their normal neurological and psychological development. Touching our children is essential for their mental health. Debating about whether we should go to them in the night is like debating about whether we should feed them when they're hungry.

Just as we distrust dependency in infancy, so do we distrust the adult sexual experience. The adult sexual experience is parallel to the human attachment process. Sexual repression in adulthood, fascination with violence, and extremes of psychopathic behavior all have their origins in lack of touch in infancy.

Some would say that it is naive to believe that we can control fate, to think that if we simply touch our children, carry them around, and respond to them with physical affection, we will protect them from harm. Of course, it is not that simple. There are no guarantees in life, much less in family life.

However, there is ample evidence in both academic studies and anecdotal experience that correlates touch, affection, and attachment in infancy with emotional stability in adulthood. Emotionally stable adults suffer all the slings and arrows of outrageous fortune, but they usually do not massacre people with rifles.

So how do we get emotionally stable adults? Let's research and publicize the studies and experiences that answer this question. Let's support efforts currently under way to educate society about the importance of the first years of life. Let's learn more about the attachment process. And let's not focus on only the intellectual potential of the early years. The intellectual potential of an individual rests on the root network of early emotional attachment.

In troubled individuals, there is often a history not only of touch used as punishment but also of poverty and lack of education. To fight violence in society, we can redouble our dedication to eliminating poverty—especially among children—and expanding educational opportunities and social programs for all. And we can learn to recognize signs of trouble.

Risk taking that is illegal, immoral, or unhealthy is a sign of trouble. Repeated unhealthy risk taking is a sign of trouble. Lack of emotional responsiveness is a sign of trouble, as is unpredictable, inconsistent, and unstable behavior. Bullying, victimizing, dominating, and shaming others are signs of trouble. Troubled individuals have no interest and make no efforts toward self-improvement, nor are they able to communicate in an uninhibited way. Other risk signs include a lack of a sense of a greater good in life, an inability to rebound from anger, and unwillingness to ask for help.

We have to look at our tolerance for violence in the media, advertising, and the legal system before we blame our children out of hand. Violence begets violence. If we want to raise nonviolent children, we have to look at what we allow them to witness, what marketing they are exposed to, and how we punish them. If we really want to look at violence in society, we have to deeply examine the way we discipline our children.

Parents are often threatened by the idea of discipline without punishment because we fear we'll give up our authority without punishment. We also fear that peaceful parenting means passive parenting. This is not necessarily so. It is, in fact, the combination of authority and mercy that helps children grow up to be nonviolent. And it's the trust and self-respect engendered by such a parenting philosophy that build self-esteem.

We have to take a long hard look at our media. It's almost impossible to protect children from premature sexuality with the explicit images that they can inadvertently access on billboards and television, in magazines and movies. The movie rating system is inconsistent and unhelpful to parents. And while the argument of free speech is often used to defend this prurient proliferation, it is license, not freedom, that allows the strong to dominate the weak for profit. This can happen only in a society without values.

Ample evidence exists about the effect of violent media on behavior, especially on the behavior of children. By the age of 12, the average child in the US may have witnessed 8,000 murders and 10,000 other acts of violence on television. Research shows that cartoon violence may have as great an impact on a young viewers as live-action violence. While the media doesn't create behavior, it does encourage it, and what it encourages are the most materialistic and superficial values at the expense of our youth.

Similar evidence exists about guns. More children are killed by firearm-related deaths in the US than in any other industrialized country. The overall firearm-related death rate among US children under the age of 15 is nearly 12 times higher than the rate among children in 25 other countries combined. For every firearm death due to self-protection, there are 37 suicides.

I defend an individual's right to bear arms, to hunt and use weapons that support a lifestyle. But like the "freedom" of pornography, the "freedom" to have excessive weapons is license in the name of freedom. I don't have the answers to gun control, but I know that we have too many guns and that we glorify them too much in cultural myth and the media.

As we all know, the media sensationalizes the darkest aspects of society. Too many deviant things get too much attention. As a parent, you know that kids will repeat behavior that is given attention. As a society, we imitate the prurient behavior that the media gives attention to. It's time to grow up.

We've been a culture in adolescence, worshipping the material world, thinking we can get along without God. Now we see the signs of our own decay. It's bad enough that we have homeless people. Intolerable that we have child kidnappers. Now we have children who kill. What can we learn from them?

Are we going to turn aside, shake our heads, and be satisfied to leave these tragedies a mystery? Or can we bear to use them to learn more about what can go wrong with our children so that we can protect them in the future?

People without conscience are inevitably dangerous to a civilized society. I don't know what to do with them. I'd like to think that as we learn more about the attachment process, we might be able to heal its disturbances. I believe in the perfectibility of the human spirit. And although I can't necessarily help the circumstances of others' lives, I can raise children in a peaceful way.

As a high school student, I debated the merits of nuclear disarmament. As a college student in the sixties, I wondered about peace. The Vietnam War confused everyone. We sat around kitchen tables drinking herb tea and talking about social change. How could we avoid war again? How does one begin with peace? Now I know that there is no way *to* peace. Peace *is* the way.

In the sixties, I believed that if I really wanted peace, I should begin with my family of birth and with myself. Later, as a parent, I valued resolving conflicts in a nonviolent way. Now I know that children are inherently peaceful unless they have been conditioned otherwise. We don't have to teach children to be peaceful, but neither must we exploit them.

Children can be harmed by lack of affection, by withholding touch, by lack of appreciation and communication, by inconsistency, unpredictability. They can suffer when no one talks to them or when they are left alone too much. Witnessing wild, uncontrollable rage on a regular basis can harm children. Children need to observe adults who have a strong sense of purpose and of a greater good in life. They need to be protected.

We can't control the fates of our children, but we can raise them in a nonviolent way. We can learn the signs of trouble in young people with impaired consciences. We can work for the modeling of less violence in society as depicted in the media. We can debate guns seriously without special interests. And we can be a society that helps parents, that loves children, that does everything possible to ensure healthy families.

From Mothering, *issue no. 89 (July–August 1998).*

parents *are* matter

RECENTLY, I PASSED A NEWSSTAND where I saw a headline
out of the corner of my eye. "Do Parents Matter?" I haven't yet
read the book to which it referred, *The Nurture Assumption*.
So I am reacting only to the headline—which is what many of
us will react to.

I've been thinking about that question for days. I'm surprised that anyone would seriously pose it, and I suspect it is
an exaggeration of the author's original intent. The fact that
we have many influences in our lives can never negate the fact
that parents do matter.

Parents matter like air and food matter. They are root
substance, cell material, DNA. They are first sounds, first
environment, first steps. They are the source matrix. Parents
are matter.

Matrix and *matter* both come from the root word *mater*,
meaning mother and measurement. In more modern times,
matrix means womb; *matter* means physical substance. The
use of the word *matter* to signify importance is fairly recent.
Matres was the Celtic Triple Goddess, or Three Fates. Matri,
or mothers, is the tantric name for all benevolent female
spirits. Matta, or Mother, is the gypsy supreme goddess. The
Gnostic or Hermetic term for matrix is *womb of matter*. This
lineage of words in dictionaries is more encouraging to read
than the popular press.

On a bad day, to read a headline suggesting that I don't
matter can be the last straw of meaninglessness that throws
me into a rage. As parents, we are busy with a myriad of

responsibilities, balancing impossible time and money challenges. To even suggest, in the midst of this exemplary effort,
that parents are superfluous is cruel.

Once again, the popular media plays on our fears and pulls
us in to be reassured about something we didn't even know
we were afraid of. Headlines like this come from collective
pessimism. Someone once said, "Optimism isn't a choice; it's
a necessity."

It's also a necessity that as a collective body we recognize
the matter of parents. At a time when initiatives for children
are on the increase, when breastfeeding is being encouraged,
and when interest in healthy living is at an all-time high, it is
discouraging to see the popular media titillate our deepest
fears about our significance as parents.

Parents receive little praise. We are hard on ourselves
and blame ourselves for everything that is wrong with our
children. If they turn out bad, we are blamed. If they turn out
good, it is because of some special gift. We're on duty seven
days a week, 24 hours a day. We deserve a better sense of
ourselves.

While our deepest fear is that we don't matter, our most
intimate moments are with our children. There is no other
relationship that has the same combination of intimacy and
trust. No relationship makes us feel quite so at ease, and none
other will challenge us as much.

Writings on attachment theory convincingly correlate
this warm intimacy between parent and child in infancy
with the adult sexual relationship. In fact, the foundations of
trust, empathy, affection, and optimism—all qualities necessary for intimacy—are laid down in the early years. Extensive
documentation supports a correlation between extreme
disruptions of this attachment period and later psychological
problems.

Other writings on human development suggest similar
critical parallels between parents and children. Joseph Chilton
Pearce, author of *Magical Child*, and Rudolf Steiner, founder
of anthroposophy, both suggest similar matrices. A matrix,
remember, is a womb, something within which something else
originates or develops. It is the material in which something is

enclosed or embedded. We carry the metaphor of the womb throughout our lives as the pattern for all future learning. We learn through a reference point, a defining context, a social fabric—a matrix.

Pearce and Steiner suggest that the matrix of the first seven years of life is the mother. In the early days, the infant doesn't know what causes discomfort. But the infant knows to seek out the mother to ease that discomfort. For the first seven years, learning is bounced off the mother. The mother is the context for learning.

The matrix of the years 7 to 14 is nature. Now the physical world, the laws and principles of nature become the deep reference point. The child bonds to the earth.

Between the years 14 and 21, the child's matrix is his or her peers. While parents decry it, children need to bond with their peers at this age, become one with them to define who they are.

At 21, young adults seek a sense of the infinite, of the ultimate, of the divine. They discover love and friendship and look for a deeper meaning in life as they enter adulthood.

The psychiatrist Erik Erikson postulated stages of life that correlate in interesting ways with the work of Pearce and Steiner. According to Erikson, the crisis of the first years of life is Trust versus Mistrust, and the outcome is Attachment. If the child is given adequate warmth, touching, love, and physical care, the child will become attached and have faith in the environment and faith in other people. On the other hand, if the care of the child is cold, indifferent, or rejecting, the child may learn to distrust the environment.

The crisis of the years one, two, and three is Autonomy and Self-Confidence versus Shame and Self-Doubt. The child who is ridiculed or overprotected when trying new skills may learn shame and self-doubt. The child who is encouraged to try new skills will develop feelings of self-control, adequacy, and independence.

Between the ages of three and five, the child learns to take initiative or to feel guilty when taking action. If the child is given the freedom to play, to ask questions, to use his or her imagination, and to choose activities, the child will learn to take initiative and to care for herself or himself. On the other hand, if the child is severely criticized, prevented from playing, or discouraged from asking questions, the child will learn to feel guilty when beginning activities, and may become immobilized when taking initiative.

The crisis of the years between 6 and 12 is Industry versus Inferiority. During these years, we learn social skills and how to be productive. When we are praised for productive activities, we learn industry. When we are criticized for being messy, childish, or inadequate, we feel inferior.

In adolescence we are developing a stable self-identity and asking the proverbial question, "Who am I?" If stable self-identity does not develop, we experience role confusion. Young adulthood is the time for forming bonds of love and friendship, and the young adult struggles with Intimacy versus Isolation.

I would base any discussion about the importance of parents and others in a child's life on these kinds of well-documented theories of human development. While it is good and true that there are multiple influences on the child, it is never true that parents don't matter. Nature would be contradictory, and she never is, if only this once in the animal kingdom, if only among humans, parents didn't matter.

Why would we even want to consider that parents don't matter? Are we looking for a way to avoid feeling so responsible? Are we overwhelmed by knowing we can never give our children everything we want, never make it perfect for them? We can guarantee very little. Sometimes it would be easier to think we don't matter than to come up against our imperfections and the inevitable unpredictability of life.

Perhaps paradox is the place of reconciliation. To endure paradox we have to have some degree of spiritual maturity. We must be able to appreciate detachment and to understand it as love in its most objective form. And we have to be able to forgive ourselves and others. Without this forgiveness, everything can be taken personally.

We have to be able to flow from one matrix to the next as life inevitably changes. As the parent of children in their early twenties, I don't yet know how to *be* the parent of adult

children. I feel like I'm starting over. And I am. I am having to
learn a whole new vocabulary. But if I thought I didn't matter,
I might just be trekking in the highlands of Nepal (not really)
or kayaking in the Hanalei River (really!).

   And then maybe I wouldn't notice the look on my 22-year-
old son's face when he comes home after being away for too
long. The way he sits in his Jeep and looks off into the moun-
tains before he drives back. Or the old friends of my kids, of
our family, who call up on Sunday afternoon to see what we're
having for dinner, who come over to visit even if my kids
aren't home. Or the traditions that have developed on their
own, the foods that must be prepared for the returning wan-
derers. These are our roots. Our environment has become
our companion.

   It all matters. We matter because of our unique expression,
not only when we're right.

   We matter and we don't. That's the paradox. We must act
as though we matter, knowing full well that all is imperma-
nent, that everything is always changing into something else.
That way we can accept that children have many influences;
that nothing is fixed; that there is always mystery. And we can
accept this without diminishing the critical role of parents in
the lives of their children—and children in the lives of their
parents.

   There's a whole web of metaphor here, a big mystery. All
the DNA, and the birth "control," and the way they turn their
heads just so. How it's perfect that they're our children, that
we're their parents, that it all makes sense and is right simply
because it is what is. All the mistakes back in the days when
we were inadvertently stupid, when we didn't know any better—all the mistakes are okay. Because the old dream was
real, and it was good even if the dream is different now. Even
though we know better now.

   From Mothering, *issue no. 91 (November–December 1998).*

what if . . . if only

SOMETIMES when we publish articles about birth, we elicit feelings of regret and self-recrimination among our readers and among our staff. When we read about "The Amazing Newborn" we wish for another baby who could crawl up our chest. When we read the history of childbirth reform, we marvel at the way politics we never knew existed contributed to our birth decisions. Even when I look at all the warm, stylin', natural clothing now available for babies, I think maybe just one more. *This time I'll get it "right."*

Regrets are funny. Why do we feel regret about some things and not about others? Obviously, the more we value something, the more we feel responsible, the more we are likely to feel regret. Or are we? Think of athletes who train for years for one special race. Can they afford to be burdened with regrets from less than perfect performances? How do they let things go?

I wonder about regrets. When I remember the past, if I did the best I knew how, looked into an issue, and made a decision based on my values and the knowledge I had at the time, then I am forgiving of my past mistakes. I even feel protective of my past ignorance. On the other hand, if I have just done something without thinking about it, or if I've known what I wanted to do but was swayed by the opinions of others, or by unexpected circumstances, I'm more likely to feel regret. I can also feel regret when I choose my own needs over another's. And on a bad day, I can feel regret about just about anything.

There are plenty of opportunities in parenthood for regrets. We are continually changing and growing as parents and with our children. Some parents regret decisions regarding circumcision or have irreconcilable differences of opinion within the family. Some regret vaccination choices because they felt pressured to make a decision. Those of us who no longer spank look back with embarrassment on our past discipline. All of us have regrets about things we feel we know better about now.

Some used birth interventions they never intended to or made decisions under pressure that they later regretted. Some wonder if their kids would have learned to spell better if they had not been homeschooled or wonder if they should have moved to a state that had better schools. There's always room for improvement. Always room for second-guessing ourselves.

In a way, second-guessing ourselves is the way we reinvent ourselves, and reinventing ourselves is the way we remain vital. Having regrets goes with the territory of taking risks. And having children is both a wonderful and a terrifying risk. Athletes learn to look at their past performance, notice what they could improve on, and then let it go. They learn not to turn against themselves in tough times and to replace negative self-talk with an encouraging and self-forgiving inner dialogue. Parents can, too.

A self-forgiving inner dialogue has its roots in an acceptance of things as they are, a larger wisdom, a bigger picture, a divine plan. And it is facilitated by the mental habit of neither inflating nor deflating ourselves. Likewise, in reconsidering the things we regret, we must negotiate between obsession and overdramatization on the one hand and avoidance and romanticization on the other.

When bad things happen or when things happen that are incongruent with our values or with who we think we are, it takes time to forgive ourselves and others.

To get forgiveness, we have to first remember what happened. Grieve over the loss, whatever it was. Give healing its own time to happen. And then, once the wound has run clear, we will have a new relationship with the past. Once self-forgiveness happens, others can be forgiven.

But how can we forgive ourselves when we have regrets about things we can't reconcile with our parenting philosophy, with our intentions? How can we let things go when the things are so important? The way to reconcile the paradoxes and the incongruities of parenthood is to believe in things exactly as they are. The only way out of endless self-recrimination as a parent is faith. It's the antidote to fear.

When is there ever not one more worthwhile thing to do? When could we not have loved just a little bit better, touched just a little bit more, investigated a difficult decision just a little bit further? I used to think that my job as a parent was to be ever better. Now I see that my job is to accept things as they are and to allow natural solutions to occur, natural rhythms to play out, natural healing to happen.

I believe in the necessity of faith because, despite my regrets, I see that my job as a parent is not to model perfection to my children but to model authenticity. They don't need to learn how to try to control things they can't control anyway. Rather, they need to learn to handle mistakes and recover from tough times. They need to learn how to do battle with such negative mental states as regret and how to opt for optimism.

I am not suggesting a smiley-face naïveté that accepts things as they are by simply dismissing the past. I don't think we change and grow that way—and the desire for self-improvement is a healthy trait. Healthy optimism looks at the past the same way we hope to look at our children's "misbehavior." We differentiate between the situation and the character of the person involved.

We talk to our child, for example, about the undesirable situation without attacking his or her character. Likewise, when we think back on things we regret, it is important not to beat ourselves up. No one wants to look at the past if they are likely to be attacked. Make looking at the past safe by accepting the integrity of your character while at the same time logically reviewing the events that you want to learn from.

It can make us nervous to trust faith. Accepting things as they are, however, is different from accepting anything that happens. How will we know if we're really off base? Are there any bells and whistles, any checklists we can review to create a framework for the trust? What is the bigger picture, the softer focus? While we're obsessing on one small detail of life with children, our life with them is happening.

In the life we have with our children, there are some traits of healthy families that are *my* bells and whistles. I like to think that even if we make some mistakes, even if we have some hard times, if these are traits that our family shares, then we are doing OK.

In healthy families, members show appreciation for one another on a regular basis. They value the unity of the family and are dedicated to promoting each other's welfare and happiness. Healthy families value communication and spend time talking with each other. When families have healthy communication skills, they feel safe talking about anything and everything. They also can more easily rebound from anger and reconcile after strong emotions.

Healthy families spend a lot of time with each other. Despite our popular myths, quality time comes from quantity time. Healthy families also have a sense of a greater good or power in life. And just as with regrets, this belief gives them strength and purpose. Interestingly enough, healthy families are not without problems. The wheel of fortune smiles and frowns on healthy families too. Healthy families, however, are able to view stress and crisis as an opportunity to grow. And healthy families ask for help.

Healthy families also are considerate. They don't victimize or shame one another. They view one another as equals. Everyone's feelings and opinions are respected. Healthy families are not dominated by one family member, be it parent or child.

If we feel that our families are generally healthy, we can let the past go, and we can work on things that we want to improve in the present. Ironically, things tend to improve on their own with trust and good example. After all, like the universe, we are ever expanding.

We can let the past go then, because it is practical to do so. How much are we willing to suffer? Sometimes our feelings of responsibility for our children are so powerful that they seem to justify a poor opinion of ourselves. We feel an empathy so deep it can be difficult to keep perspective.

If what I do with my children is of such importance, how can I forgive my transgressions? Because I must. A healthy person, mother of a healthy family, does not wallow in her perceived imperfections. It is a bad example. It's as if we must make a contract with optimism. We give our children the birthright of optimism in the early years. They give us back this optimism throughout the ever-changing symphony of family life. I can forgive my own transgressions because along with the precious fragility of the human child comes a tremendous resilience. Life has hardwired us for survival, and while simply surviving is not optimal, it illustrates how benign the universe really is.

Being a parent is a whole lot easier when we're in a good mood. We hardly ever beat ourselves up about what we did or didn't do in the past right after a funny movie and a great dinner or a rollicking wrestle on the floor with the kids or a relaxing vacation. If anything, the urge to regret is a signal to take a nap. The trap of thinking we can actually do all the good deeds we think of for our children is wide and deep.

So we choose. We choose how much we want to suffer, even for a good cause, even for those we love the most. In the face of serious unhappiness caused by regrets from the past, ask yourself these questions:

How much of this do I want to feel? How long do I want to feel this way? What is good about this situation? What can I learn from what has happened? How can I prevent it from happening in the future? How can I make this work for me?

To lift yourself from hyperfocus on the past to participation in the present, ask yourself: What am I looking forward to? What am I grateful for in my life?

When we ask these questions we begin to see that we have a relationship with our moods and perceptions that we can change. We can decrease our willingness to suffer. We can act happy. Find an excuse to laugh. Just raising up the corners of our mouths in a smile can lift our mood. All of the intellectual arguments about what happened in the past pale in comparison to the immediacy with which a good laugh can change our mood and thus our perspective.

In fact, people at every age report the same levels of happiness. We recover from tragedy fairly quickly. We're much more resilient than we believe. Happiness can be found both from momentary joy and lasting contentment. Regrets can prove to be strong, however, when we don't feel we have control over our environment. So getting that sense of control is one of the cornerstones of happiness. People are happy if they are optimistic, just as optimists are spurred on by defeat. Faith is a quality that happy people share. They are fortunate to have meaningful activity and close relationships.

I wonder when we rehash our regrets, if our children care at all about our foibles. What is our legacy to them, after all? I hope that it's all the right things. But in the event that it's not, what true legacy can I really guarantee? If I can guarantee it, it must somehow be all that is really needed.

I can guarantee the modeling of authentic behavior, albeit with ever-evolving, starting-over techniques. And some misbehavior. Some serious optimism. Still, I can't control the destinies of my children. I have to give them up to life. Life will happen to them as it happens to all of us—despite our best intentions, despite our protestations.

I cannot give them everything. I can give them forgiveness. And I can give them faith. And I can give them resilience.

From Mothering, *issue no. 92 (January–February 1999).*

getting bigger

BECOMING A PARENT is really much more than most of us bargained for. Who knew that what seemed like a simple love affair with our baby would turn into such a major personal transformation? Who knew that having a child would require us to get so much bigger?

It's funny that even as we continually witness our children getting bigger, we seldom realize that we are getting bigger along with them. I once heard someone say that women move forward by going deeper. That seems to me the way it is. As we grow up with our children, we do so by going deeper.

And how do we go deeper? Well, for one thing, we begin to examine comfortable assumptions. Having a baby requires us to look at life through new filters; and our previous assumptions, beliefs, and attitudes all come up for review.

Before becoming pregnant, one may be influenced, for example, by the horror stories of others or the unrealistic media portrayals of birth and think that birth is a medical event, that birth is scary. Once you become pregnant, however, and feel the mommy hormones course through your bloodstream, you begin to question this blanket fear of birth and to realize that birth is actually normal, simple, and as safe as life gets.

Coming to such a radical belief involves a personal transformation. We have to transform our own fear of birth into a powerful relationship with birth. In other words, we have to trust our inherent capacity to know how to respond to birth, to know how to respond to the unknown.

Birth is just the first of the countless times we will confront the fear of the unknown for the love of our child. Often we feel the need for a script, a philosophy, a book, a guru. Certainly we can't face this unknown world of life with our child without some rules. Certainly we can't just go our own way.

But we must. All of evolution depends on us going our own way. Genius, by the way, only happens as a happy accident. It can't be predicted or manipulated. It just happens. It must be, therefore, that what seem like happy accidents are, in fact, grand schemes. There must be, after all, a script of which our own intuition is the only author.

Dancer and choreographer Martha Graham says it best: "There is a vitality, a life-force, an energy, a quickening, that is translated through you into action, and because there is only one of you in all of time, this expression is unique. And if you block it, it will never exist through any other medium and be lost. The world will not have it. It is not your business to determine how good it is nor how valuable nor how it compares to other expressions. It is your business to keep it yours clearly and directly, to keep the channel open. You have to keep open and aware directly to the urges that motivate you. Keep the channel open."

Since first reading this quote, I have spent a lot of time thinking about what "one of you in all of time" actually means. Never again. Never before. Only once in all of time past, present, or future has there been and will there be a you, a me, your crazy child, my nutty friend. What an enormous responsibility. It must be so then, if this is true, that this is our responsibility. It is our responsibility to answer to our inner, unique yearnings, to direct our own lives, follow our own script. It must mean that when in doubt, we must trust ourselves. It must be true that "deep down" we do know.

So this is what "getting bigger" as a parent is all about. It's about trusting ourselves because there is only one of us. Trusting our intuition and experience as much as, if not more than, any quantification or analysis. Trusting the subjective; trusting the self.

When you think about it, you realize that you have a visceral bond with your child. You are of the same matter. And you realize that there is a psychic link that mother and infant share in utero that continues throughout life. For parents, the bond with our children is a cellular one that stretches from beginning to end. We know more than we realize.

It's easy to say that we know best, that we should trust ourselves, that we are unique, that we understand what's best for ourselves and our family. That sounds good; everyone would probably agree with it. But it's much easier said than done. Simply put, trusting yourself means having confidence in yourself. And how do we get confidence in ourselves as parents when we are in a totally improvisational position?

We get confidence by showing up. No script or book or great expert can protect us from suffering. We have to go the way alone; we can't get out of it. We are the one in charge. Trying to protect ourselves from suffering by following a way will not protect us. Only taking responsibility will protect us. Taking responsibility is such an act of bravery that it perpetuates courage. That is the way it always is. We get courage by being brave.

The woman who chooses homebirth is brave. She feels the simple safety of birth inside her, and while she cannot help but be influenced by those who doubt this safety, she knows that she must choose. She will birth best wherever she feels safe.

The woman who chooses to breastfeed in difficult situations and in everyday situations in which breastfeeding is challenged, she, too, is brave. Simple acts of bravery by simple mothers who follow their hearts inspire courage that serves them well their whole lives. Being a mother is powerful not only because everything begins with the mother, but because it uncovers in her new reservoirs of patience, humility, and trust.

Trust is important because it underlies all decisions we make. But why is it an issue? Why don't we just trust ourselves automatically? Our children do. They trust themselves, sometimes to our dismay. They have a deep personal integrity.

Let's take birth, for example. In the US, we tend to believe that hospital birth is most common. In fact, homebirth is more common in the world as a whole, and research shows that birth is safe in any setting. It is safe at home, in a birth center, and at a hospital. Our beliefs are often based on assumptions rather than facts. We must reexamine them for the sake of our children. This is what makes us bigger.

Before we have children, we are in fact children ourselves, children of the culture. When we become parents, we become the culture. We become an adult in the eyes of the community. And as such, where we once allowed authoritative knowledge to reside in others—in the expert, in our parents, in the state—we now must allow authority to take up residence within the self, within ourselves.

And just as we allow authority to reside in ourselves, so must we have renewed trust and faith in life itself. To do our jobs best as parents, we must believe in the perfectibility of life. We must be optimistic. We must see the world as a benign universe.

Although most of us would say, in fact, that we fear and distrust some aspects of modern society, most of us trust ourselves to it every day. We entrust our lives to strangers on highways and depend every day on people we'll never know for our food, power, and transportation. We do trust the world on a regular basis, and most of the time it's trustworthy.

We can enhance our own trust in ourselves by adding some of these tools for better living to our parenting repertoire:

- While it's almost impossible as a parent to get much time alone, it is possible to find a few minutes to think. Ten minutes a day for meditation is a worthwhile goal. Walks in nature with your baby in the backpack are a way to let your thoughts wander.
- Read some books on normal human development, normal psychological development. Talk to older people about children. Educate yourself on the most progressive, open-minded, and time-tested views of normal childhood.
- Read *The Traits of a Healthy Family* by Dolores Curran.
- Develop new communication skills.
- Learn coping mechanisms for tough times.
- Understand that change and the personal transformation of parenthood take time, and be gentle with yourself as you continually change alongside your children.

It sounds simple to advocate that we be gentle on ourselves as we change, but what does that mean, and how important can it really be? It's essential. If we are to say that the authority for intuitive, authentic decisions about our child's well-being rests in us, then we must support and strengthen ourselves with great attentiveness. Ironically, the kinder we are to ourselves, the more we will believe in ourselves.

Again, there is no prolonged free time when one is a parent, but there are 15 minutes. Here are some things you can do in 15 minutes that will allow you to catch your breath and settle your mind:

- Walk outside
- Go to a park
- Go for a walk
- Take a bath
- Call a friend
- Read a poem
- Have a cup of tea
- Look at the clouds
- Lie in the hammock
- Sit by the fire
- Sit by the window
- Lie in the grass
- Lie on the floor

When we are tired all the time, easily angry, on the verge of tears, or afraid of everything, we need to rest. We cannot expect ourselves to make important decisions regarding our children when we are not at our best. Sometimes we don't realize how the simple solutions of enough sleep, good food, and some unstructured time for relaxation can make most problems disappear.

Being gentle with ourselves also means having the good sense to allow ourselves to catch our breath and think things through. Trusting ourselves means appreciating that we sometimes need more information. Making decisions in our own way and at our own speed gives us the time to complete deep decision making.

This deep decision making is part of getting to know ourselves. It is what keeps us getting bigger as we face the new challenges that our children continually bring to our lives. Deep decision making is also how we learn to trust ourselves, because self-knowledge, the foundation of deep decision making, is also the foundation of self-trust.

Self-knowledge also allows us to appreciate our limitations as well as our strengths. Even while we claim our authority as parents, even while we make decisions in the most authentic and original way we know how, we don't have to be right. We just have to be ourselves. That is our greatest security.

From Mothering, *issue no. 94 (May–June 1999).*

your will—mine

I AWOKE THIS MORNING to the smell of smoke in the air. I knew at once what it was. A forest fire is burning about 20 miles to the northeast of our land. Three days ago, I watched a huge cloud of smoke form above the mountain behind my house. The last few evenings I've seen helicopters fly back and forth across the canyon, bringing water to the fire. This morning it was slurry bombers wending their way above us every 15 minutes. New Mexico is burning.

I live in a ponderosa pine forest. In the last month there have been four major forest fires in our state: one 45 miles west of here in Los Alamos and Santa Fe National Forest and two 200 miles south at different locations in the Lincoln National Forest. This new one, in the Pecos Wilderness, is just a few ridges away from me, but not close enough to actually be a threat to us.

The children and I have already talked about what we would take with us if we had to flee the house. Not very much, really. Old family photos, albums, mementos, my books of poems. Pretty much everything else is replaceable. Of those who lost their homes to the 48,000-acre fire that destroyed much of Los Alamos, most said they were just grateful that they and their loved ones were unharmed. Tragedy underlines what is really important in life.

In tragedy, such as the fires in New Mexico, one appreciates the simple things. As I listen to the slurry bombers fly over my house, I water the garden. It helps me counter the drought. I make the gardens beautiful with straw and wood chips. I get such joy from playing in the water, doing what I want to do outside. There's a kind of joyful recharge that comes from wandering, meandering, being spontaneously self-directed. That's why we call it play.

Self-direction is one of the great values of play. We all enjoy it. Children love to—need to—play. This is how they create themselves. They practice different realities in play and from them form a personality. It is easy for parents to forget the importance of simple, unstructured play because of the pressures we all feel to make sure that our children have all the appropriate advantages. The greatest advantage to childhood, however, may simply be free time.

When my children were young, there was a growing number of programs for children. Now there are endless choices of dance, music, art, sports, drama, martial arts, gymnastics, yoga, etc. for children of all ages. Many parents feel pressured for their children to compete with other children for excellence and achievement in these and other pursuits. We often feel in competition with other parents. We also feel pressure to begin our children in formal educational programs at younger and younger ages, and for longer and longer periods.

While it is important that children and families interact with their peers and take advantage of appropriate learning opportunities, it is also essential for us not to expect of our children too much abstract learning in their first three to five years. This is when they are learning from the home environment, digging in the dirt of themselves. This is their matrix, their focal point of learning, during these early years.

While early childhood education is right for some children, it is not necessary for all children. Don't forget that it was first created for children whose home environments were compromised. The home environment is superior for learning during the early years.

My children are now 18 through 26, and they were all home at once recently. On that occasion, I lay in my bed at night beaming, as I counted one, two, three, four—just as I used to before we crossed the street together when they were little. While they were all here, my daughter found an audiotape of their voices when they were six months through eight years old.

They were amazed to hear their own young voices. Hearing

the games they played and their interactions took me back. I
had remembered well their dear, sweet voices, and while they
delighted me, what amazed me most was my recollection of
the intensity of those early, busy years with the children. The
noise of their play resounds even now. I wrote this poem when
they were all at home recently:

just a glance

I can tell
My kids apart
From the back
Of their heads,
The nape
Of their necks,
The curve of
Their hands as
They wrap
Their fingers
Around mine.
They are older
Now,
But still the laughter
Of their rowdy
Play
Echoes
Through the house.
They dug deeply
In the earth then.
They drew sweetly from
Themselves.
They feast now
On the fruits of
That foundation.

That recording my children found not only recalled the
intensity of my early years with children, but it also reminded
me of how earnest I have been. When the children were
younger, I felt that I was preparing them for something,
thought that I had better make sure they took advantage of the

right opportunities, realized their potential. I'm still unsure if I've done that—if I could have. I know now, as I did not with my first, that we're always realizing our potential. We don't just get done with it. Even with adult children, I still have dreams, uncertainties, regrets—and plans for them.

I remember in the movie *Parenthood* when the older father tells his son, also a father, that parenthood is not like reaching the goal line. After all, we never reach the line. There's no end. We're always playing the game. I like that. It keeps giving me more chances to get it right. But not right like creating a product, a certain result. Right like correct.

It is not correct for us to make our children in our own likeness. It is correct for us to facilitate their own likenesses. I am reminded of the words of Kahlil Gibran in *The Prophet:*

> *Your children are not your children,*
> *They are the sons and daughters of Life's longing for itself,*
> *They come through you but not from you,*
> *And though they are with you yet they belong not to you.*
> *You may give them your love but not your thoughts,*
> *For they have their own thoughts.*
> *You may house their bodies but not their souls,*
> *For their souls dwell in the house of tomorrow, which*
> *you cannot visit, not even in your dreams.*
> *You may strive to be like them, but seek not to make*
> *them like you,*
> *For life goes not backward nor tarries with yesterday.*

Just as we cannot make our children in our image, so we cannot prepare them for everything. There will always be the unexpected. The best antidote to the unexpected is the capacity to improvise, and that capacity is rooted in an ability to trust our own inner authority. We can give our children that. We parents must not handicap them with the belief that authority rests outside of themselves—in friends, teachers, sweethearts, parents, scientists, journalists, politicians. We can demonstrate to our children that authority resides within each of them by raising them to believe in themselves.

What is the correct balance between imposing our author-

ity, our will, on our children, and facilitating each child's own
authority, or will? There is no one way to answer this question.
There is always a dance. A push and pull. It changes with the
ages and growth of our children and with our own capacity and current persuasion. This correct balance mirrors the
natural world, where learning happens through interaction. In
other words, the world and our relationships are self-learning
tools. They teach us what we need to know.

Children learn about the natural world and thus about
themselves by having opportunities for unstructured time and
self-directed play. It is easy to confuse our own lost ambitions
for ourselves with our ambitions for our children. Who wants
to play the piano? Who always wanted to be a dancer? We can
learn to love our children as they are, not as we want them
to be. This doesn't mean that we give up our dreams of our
child's greatest possibility, but we also live happily with what
is. That's the dance.

And it's the dance that is the point. We believe that we are
teaching our children how to do this or that, when in fact we
are teaching them how to be. They often learn more from how
we solve problems, how we interact, how we rebound than
from the fleeting information we offer. It is moments that are
unforgettable. The feeling of the moment is what creates the
memory.

What we remember, what we treasure in the end, are the
spontaneous, intimate moments when we feel connected with
a beloved human being. It is the mementos of those moments
that we keep in case of tragedy, that we treasure in life. We
remember at those times that we are already always living a
miracle. How wonderful just to remember this and to give
thanks.

Now that my children are grown, I see the wonderful roots
of their childhoods bearing fruit. I see how those early years
with them were hard because they were digging their foundations. Twenty-two years ago, I wrote this poem. It has turned
out to be true:

there will be time

There is time still
for sitting in cafés
in Paris
sipping wine.
Time still
for going to meet
The guru.
There is time still.
Now I am caring for eternity.
Carrying bodies soft with sleep
to beds of flowered
quilts and pillows.
Answering cries deep out of
nighttime fears.
Buckling shoes.
Opening doors.
Pretending.
My soul now is dwelling in
the house of tomorrow.
Tomorrow there will be time
for long leisurely conversations,
For poems to write,
And dances to perform.
Time still.
So I surrender now
to them and this,
Knowing it is they
who will teach me
how to do it all.

From Mothering, *issue no. 101 (July–August 2000).*

it's not your fault

EARLY THIS MORNING I was awakened by the squawking of
ravens. After tossing and turning for a while and trying to fall
back to sleep, I decided to just get up and have a bath. Maybe
a hot lavender bath would help me relax, I thought. It worked.
I fell asleep for several hours after the bath, even though the
ravens continued to serenade.

I was having trouble falling back to sleep this morning
because I was reworking in my mind disagreements and hurt
feelings from the night before. I had had an argument with
one of my daughters and a misunderstanding with another.
Both incidents had caused withdrawal, and we had not as yet
rebounded from our anger.

Although I thought that I was the one with the hurt feelings, I still blamed myself. Causing pain to those we love is
in such contrast to what we want that when it happens, we
can be overcome with self-recrimination regardless of the
circumstances.

Self-recrimination implies that we have control over inter-
personal relationships, but we do not. It may seem that when
everything is running smoothly in the family, it is because of
something that we did. When things go poorly, however, we
realize that this is not always so. While the will and actions of
our own personal lives must certainly be directed toward our
own perfectibility, the larger life of the society in which we
participate is inherently out of our control. This is because
we are part of a larger pattern, one that we cannot easily
orchestrate.

Even so, once there has been conflict with a loved one, it is normal to blame ourselves. When we do this, we review our own behavior and that of our child, and eventually we get perspective and recover. For a while, though, it's as if we have had the rug pulled out from under us.

If we're lucky, as we recover from conflict, we also begin to reconcile with our child. This morning—after the bath and the nap—my daughter came into my room on her knees carrying a flower. She apologized for yesterday.

With my other daughter, it was a more reluctant reconciliation at first, and then fast and easy. We just couldn't stay mad at each other.

Such reconciliations after anger help us fully recover from the experience and often, if not always, cause us to go deeper with one another. In fact, a child's crisis of need often results in going deeper with ourselves and thus with each other and in that way is a corrective to our relationship.

Marriage is another example of a relationship in which this type of correction is common. Marriages have crises of intimacy that allow the marriage to mature. Recently, a friend called to tell me that she and her husband had gotten very angry with one another. To her surprise, after their anger had dissipated, they were physically and emotionally more intimate. They went deeper.

Sometimes our children signal their need to go deeper with us in confusing ways. Another friend has two young boys close in age. Her son's teacher called her recently to ask if anything was wrong at home because he'd been acting sad. After spending more time with her son and reviewing her behavior with him, my friend wondered if he got as much attention as her oldest son did. She was also concerned that perhaps his older brother dominated him. And she blamed herself. She wondered if her son's sad feelings were because of something she was—or was not—doing.

These are healthy questions to ask because perhaps there is something different that her son needs now. Maybe his behavior is his way of communicating to her, since his verbal skills and self-reflection are not as well developed. My friend will review her personal dynamic with her son and his dynamic with the family, and together they will make a correction. Sometimes our relationship with our children grows nice and easy like a summer day; other times it changes as dramatically as a winter blizzard and can blow us away.

Regardless of the temperature, however, disturbances in the emotional climate of our home often facilitate increased closeness. To sail through them, we go deeper. While guilt and self-recrimination may sometimes be by-products of these conflicts, increased intimacy is almost always the result. Even with people we don't particularly like, conflict can increase intimacy.

Often it's our own selves with whom we need to increase intimacy. And our children sometimes act needy because they recognize that we are off balance. Like all overworked, over-tired, worried parents, when we saturate our capacity, we can be more reactive to our children's behavior than we might be at other times. In fact, it is usually a combination of a child's legitimate need and our own legitimate personal limitations that leads to conflict. Such is life.

When we are emotionally out of balance, our children sometimes become needy because they can sense that something is wrong but don't understand what it is. Their desire for a correction in behavior not only comes from their own needs but is also related to our level of responsiveness. When our level of responsiveness changes or their needs change, our children often let us know through their behavior. Behavior is, in fact, their language.

But what language or rebounding can there be with older children, especially when things are more difficult—when, for example, our children's behavior does not meet our expectations? Perhaps we love sports, and our children are not interested. We love to read, and they love to watch TV. We know they have a gift for music, but they're not interested in lessons. In other words, they just do not always want what we want for them or even what we think they need, and coercing them can create problems.

For some, it is more than simply having different interests. In many families, children follow different educational or vocational paths than their parents had hoped for them.

This is one area we feel very serious about as parents, and it can be difficult to support our adult children when they make choices that we believe may not be in their own best interests. I believe that it takes young adults a lot longer to "find themselves" than we would like to believe—perhaps the entire decade of their 20s. They say that great talents blossom late, yet we desperately want to be reassured that our grown-up children will be OK out in the world.

My own daughter decided at the end of her second year of high school that she just could not continue to go to the school she was attending. She had lost interest in learning and did not consider herself competent. Because of the confidence in learning that I had gained from homeschooling this child and my others, it was not too difficult for me to agree to her wishes, although she made it perfectly clear that it was not my decision. I insisted, though, that she do this only in conjunction with a larger plan for getting her GED and going to the community college. Still, I have trepidation about her path.

Most of us expect our children to follow our own paths to a large extent. If we went to college, we expect that our children will follow. I find, however, that it's a different world now. When I went to college, I could expect a certain kind of job and level of income. This expectation is less certain at this time in history. While college assuredly has great benefits, it is no longer a guarantee of success, and our children know this. Often they choose more experiential learning.

My daughter did go on to get her GED and to take courses at the community college. And now she is interested in college. The unique and individual choices that she has made will require that she find a unique and individual way to attend college, however. I sometimes blame myself for this situation because I have chosen to reside in a community that does not have good public junior and senior high schools. I live in a poor state that does not allocate sufficient resources to education. While I love where I live and where I have raised my children, I sometimes wonder if this choice has handicapped them. I blame myself.

Others suffer much more. My suffering over my unmet

expectations for my children pales in comparison to those whose children have taken dangerous courses or been victimized. One wonderful family I know that has done "everything right" suffers because an adult child struggles with drug addiction. Another woman, pioneer of birth reform in the US, suffers with the same burden. Friends of my parents lost a son to suicide. Another mother, a La Leche League leader and international speaker, suffers the unspeakable. Her adult child was murdered. I bow to the burdens of these parents: "There but for the grace of God go I." And, contrary to what we sometimes tell ourselves in moments of self-recrimination, bad things do happen to healthy families.

Could any of these healthy families have prevented the suffering and tragedy of their children's lives? Can any of us prevent our children from suffering? Could the parents who marched in the Million Mom March in memory of their slain children have prevented their deaths? I think not.

In our zealousness as new parents, we think we can protect our children from all ills. Further, we believe that our children miraculously spring from us complete with our seasoned knowledge and thus will not have to repeat our mistakes. We don't realize that these "mistakes" are the necessary building blocks of human development.

One of the tenets of human development is that we cannot control the experiences of others, even our children. As they grow older this becomes increasingly so. And yet, in an esoteric way, we are always responsible for them because we created them. We brought them into the world. Therefore, while we are not always to blame for their behavior, we are correct to feel responsible. Herein lies our anguish.

In all situations of conflict, either conflict with our children or conflict among them, our anguish is our teacher. It teaches us to correct our behavior when appropriate and to surrender to the larger mystery when there is nothing we can do. Knowing the difference is our life's work as parents. We never get to the end of this work. It is the practice of a lifetime.

As parents who are self-reflective human beings, we will always seek to correct our behavior if necessary. And we hope to forgive ourselves when we have done all we can. Our children correct our course and that of the family better than anyone else does. They see us without filters. They are spontaneous. They adore us. Our children can level us like no one else. But when they do, they pick us up off the floor with the most gentle hands.

From Mothering, *issue no. 102 (September–October 2000).*

compatibility

FOR THE LAST TWO YEARS, I have been trying to figure
out the cause of my allergic symptoms: swelling, dryness,
and itching. While I've been cared for by fine practitioners
and have been involved in helpful treatment plans, I am still
the one who has to manage the situation and the sometimes
contradictory diagnoses. Even with good care, I am the one
ultimately responsible for my health.

I hear the stories of many parents who are treated by
health professionals in an adversarial manner because they
want to be the ones to make the final decisions regarding their
child's health care, because they want a second opinion, or
because they want to use integrative medicine. And yet if we
as parents give up our authority, we would be irresponsible.

One mother I know noticed dark spots on her toddler's
teeth and took her to a pediatrician, who told her that her
baby would need dental work. The dentist she went to wiped
the dark spots off her daughter's teeth with a cloth and told
the mother not to give her any more cereal with iron. Another
mother whose toddler actually had cavities was told to stop
breastfeeding immediately. A second opinion revealed that
breastmilk is not, in fact, a cause of decay because breastmilk
is sucked and swallowed at the same time and does not pool
in the mouth. She found another dentist who understood this
situation and filled her daughter's teeth without "requiring"
weaning.

Both these mothers worried greatly over the conflicting
opinions, but they made their own choices and were happy

to have practitioners with whom they felt compatible. Other mothers are not so lucky. Some families who make choices not to vaccinate, to refuse prenatal testing, or to question HIV drug treatment or cancer treatment are threatened with the loss of custody of their children if they do not comply with standard practice and state laws.

This is unconscionable in light of the fact that standard practice changes decade to decade, and scientific thought, by nature, is always evolving. In the 1970s, silver nitrate was routinely used as an eye prophylaxis for newborn babies. Many parents refused it because it blurred the baby's eyesight during the sensitive bonding period. Today, erythromycin is the eye prophylaxis of choice. In the 1950s, X-rays were used commonly with children. Today, we know that they should be used sparingly.

It is unethical, if not downright illegal, to coerce someone to receive treatment that they conscientiously object to. There seems to be an alarming increase in efforts to dissuade individuals from making choices of conscience regarding health care and a growing misconception that individual freedom of choice is at odds with the common good.

Both the political climate as well as the restrictive and expensive nature of health care in the US underscore the importance of taking charge of our own health and the health of our children. By this, I don't mean running away to the woods and abandoning modern medicine. On the contrary, modern medicine should be used in an integrated way in conjunction with all appropriate modalities and with final decision making resting in the hands of the individual.

Just because a procedure or drug is available is not always a compelling enough reason to use it. We must also feel that it is appropriate for our child and that it is considered in the context of everything that is good for the child. For example, a parent whose child is in remission from leukemia may want to postpone chemotherapy and reevaluate it based on the child's progress. From a parent's view, this makes perfect sense. From the public health view, it is heresy.

This inevitable conflict emphasizes the importance of the relationship we have with our health care practitioner. If we have a relationship that is unequal and authoritative, we will feel reluctant to discuss our values and our fears. We may prefer a practitioner with whom we can collaborate and who will tolerate our choices even if they are idiosyncratic.

This kind of collaboration can be found with practitioners of all persuasions. We should not assume that collaboration is possible only with alternative-minded practitioners. Traditional, allopathic practitioners—as well as alternative, complementary, and integrative practitioners—can understand this type of collaboration, and yet they can be hard to find. I discovered that these types of practitioners became easier to find once I was willing to take responsibility for my own health care.

In addition to a willingness to collaborate, we want practitioners who share our values. Sometimes we think that if we explain ourselves well, we will be understood by practitioners who have different values from our own, but there is no guarantee of this, and different values can indicate an inherent incompatibility.

The importance of the issue of inherent compatibility is perhaps best illustrated with regard to our choice of the practitioner to be with us at the birth of our baby. We will get the type of birth that he or she specializes in. We naively assume that if we write a great birth plan and present this to our practitioner, all will go our way. This is not always so. If our practitioner shares our values and already incorporates the practices "requested" in our birth plan into his or her own practice, then things will more likely go our way. If, however, the things that we value are uncommon in the practice or the setting where birth will take place, then the likelihood of things going our way diminishes. It is as if we've gone into a restaurant that routinely serves fish and chips and fried food and ordered a salad. We may get a salad, but it is unlikely that it will be the salad we had in mind, and it may include side dishes we never even knew were on the menu.

However, even when we find compatible practitioners, we cannot abdicate responsibility for our own health or the health of our children. We still have to make the final decisions. Will it be antibiotics or not? Will we add some vitamin

C, echinacea, and zinc? How about some mullein ear drops? Maybe some chicken or miso soup. A humidifier might help. Acidophilus and probiotics will be good after the antibiotics to rebuild the intestinal flora. Many of these complements to drug treatment are home remedies that parents have been using for years and that have only recently gotten the medical stamp of approval. Unlike the FDA and other agencies, we don't have to wait for approval. We know when something works.

The process of discovering which remedies are effective for individuals and for family members, as well as the act of taking responsibility for our health, is greatly enhanced by accessing our intuition. I've found that in trying to discover the cause of my own sensitivities, I've had to develop my intuition, because it is my intuition that helps me sort out the sometimes contradictory information provided by my different health care "consultants."

I believe that we have an inner sense of self-protection and a fierce protectiveness for our children. We can't give ourselves or our children up to anyone's care without understanding it and monitoring it, without managing it. In a way, then, health care professionals do become our "consultants."

It is this idea of consultation that underlies the tradition of informed consent. I have been thinking a lot about informed consent lately, in view of stories I have mentioned before about parents who have had custody of their children threatened because they held minority viewpoints on health care. Certainly, there are rare cases where a parent's extreme beliefs threaten the health of their child, but parents who hold minority health care beliefs are usually exceptionally well informed. Minority viewpoints should not be summarily dismissed, as it is the minority opinion that grows into the majority view.

When *Mothering* questioned routine medical circumcision 22 years ago, we were considered mad, but today the pediatric medical associations of Canada, the UK, Australia, and the US have published statements opposed to routine medical circumcision. When we questioned antibiotics 15 years ago, we were considered mad, but while they are still frequently prescribed today, it is common knowledge that they can be overused. When parents question antibiotics or other drug therapies, or when they decline routine newborn testing or new vaccinations, they do so with the full support of the Bill of Rights and the traditions of jurisprudence.

For nearly 100 years in the US, we have recognized the tradition of informed consent. It is more accurate, however, to use the term informed choice. Consent implies authority; choice implies equality. Instead of assuming that blanket consent forms constitute informed choice or waiting for the practitioner to inform us, we can ask the questions that are required for us to make a choice. Prior to all treatments— allopathic, alternative, complementary, integrative—we should be able to reflect on the following things:

- A complete description of the treatment
- The benefits of the treatment/drug
- The risks of the treatment/drug
- The alternatives to this treatment/drug

We should not feel coerced into making a decision, and we should have the choice to do nothing at all. Many of us feel coerced into treatment for our babies. We feel coerced to give medicines we question, and we do not feel safe asking questions about commonly accepted practices such as vaccinations, ear tubes, dental sealants, mercury fillings, and antibiotics. We want the advice of health care professionals, but we do not want to be humiliated or patronized when we ask legitimate questions.

It is a rocky time in health care. The US medical-pharmaceutical industry has made illness into a business, and as a result, we're often compromised regarding our health. By finding practitioners who share our values or respect us despite our differences, we can breathe a sigh of relief.

I have learned this the hard way. My son was born with a birth defect that required several surgeries during his infancy. My requests to be with him in the hospital were met with ridicule by one well-respected plastic surgeon. As a young mother intimidated by the medical profession, I didn't know what to do, but I refused to accept this opinion. My presence was not negotiable. Sure enough, I found another, even more well-

respected plastic surgeon who openly accepted and accommodated my concerns. However, the nurses in the hospital
were less enthusiastic about my presence, and once again I
was considered mad.

Ironically, by the time my five-month-old daughter was
hospitalized with spinal meningitis four years later, rooming in
was routine. I was no longer considered the mad mother but
rather a helpful part of the health care team.

Through my experience, I learned that I cannot abandon
my health or that of my children to pills and platitudes. I cannot assume that following the doctor's "orders" is always right.
I have to make sure that the doctor's "orders" do not conflict
with my orders. I have been entrusted with this child. I must
be the one who knows. The knowledge must be in me. Otherwise, this gift of faith who is my child would not be safe. I
must not abandon my inherent responsibility, even if it means
losing social mileage, looking like a fool, or making a mistake.
My orders precede the doctor's. I am, after all, the mother.

From Mothering, *issue no. 104 (January–February 2001).*

resist much, obey little

BEFORE I BECAME A MOTHER, I believed that authority rested outside of myself. Once I had children, however, I realized that my authority as a parent was based not on my experience but on my position. The authority lies with my own inherent wisdom, my own inherent expertise as a mother. This authority is not based on the fact that I know everything. Often, in fact, I do not. My authority as a mother rests not on being right but on the fact that I am the mother.

This authority is often undermined by overarching societal beliefs that assume authoritative knowledge to be outside of oneself. And it is specifically undermined when those in positions of authority make universal recommendations for families in the absence of their input.

This type of one-sided recommendation was made in the fall of 1999, just two years after the American Academy of Pediatrics (AAP) issued its historic probreastfeeding statement. That year the organization published *Guide to Your Child's Sleep*, a book that effectively undermines successful breastfeeding by raising doubts about the legitimacy of infants' nighttime needs and by engendering fear about cosleeping. Cosleeping is a common international practice that makes breastfeeding easier and thus more successful.

Parental authority will again be undermined by an upcoming recommendation of the AAP. The recommendation that all infants receive vitamin D supplementation beginning at two months of age is based on an increase of rickets in the US. Rickets is a deficiency disease that affects the young during the period of skeletal growth and is characterized by soft and deformed bones. It's caused by a vitamin D deficiency; vitamin D helps the body absorb calcium and phosphorus. These new cases of rickets occur in populations that routinely cover a large part of their bodies or live in areas where it's unsafe to go outside.

Apparently, the AAP refuses to recommend sun exposure because of the risk of skin cancer. Rather than identifying populations at risk for rickets, excluding breastfed babies from the recommendation, or encouraging governmental attention to the environment, the organization has chosen instead to recommend that all babies in the US receive a synthetic version of vitamin D made by a formula manufacturer.

According to the 1997 AAP statement, "Breastfeeding should be the sole food for baby for the first six months. After that, breastfeeding should continue for at least a year along with complementary food." How could the AAP have changed its mind so quickly after its historic 1997 statement? If it is true that breastfed babies need to be supplemented with a vitamin at two months of age, then what else might breastmilk be missing? This recommendation intentionally raises questions about the integrity of breastmilk.

I remember in the 1970s when questions were raised about the integrity of breastmilk because research had not yet caught up with what nature and mothers knew all along. It was believed then that there was not enough iron in breastmilk, and it was commonly recommended that all babies begin solids at four months. Research later showed, of course, that although human milk does not contain large amounts of iron, it does contain the right proportion of lactose and vitamin C to promote excellent iron absorption. In fact, 49 percent of the iron in breastmilk is absorbed, while only 4 percent of the iron in cow's milk is. Will we learn years from now that vitamin D is more available in breastmilk than we originally thought?

It undermines breastfeeding to suggest that breastmilk is the perfect infant food except for . . . iron . . . or vitamin D. What will it be next? DHA is on the horizon. This pendulum swing of medical opinion seriously undermines a mother's confidence in her own body and her own inherent wisdom as a mother.

The AAP recommendation further challenges breastfeeding because it undermines the concept of exclusive breastfeeding. It has taken almost 30 years of advocacy work to change the US recommendation for solid foods from four to six months. Suggesting that breastmilk is not sufficient unto itself and that anything else is needed before six months opens the door for further undermining confidence in breastmilk.

The gut of the exclusively breastfed baby is different from the gut of a baby who has had anything else. The gut is changed by the addition of formula, by solid foods, and by vitamin supplementation. Research like that which we highlight in our HIV articles would have been impossible if all babies were routinely supplemented. Exclusive breastfeeding is an important concept in breastfeeding research and advocacy and in natural family planning and is eroded by this recommendation.

I would like the AAP to speak to the larger implications of its recommendation. I find it hard to believe that the few minutes of daily sun necessary to allay or prevent rickets constitute a cancer risk. And if the organization believes its research to such an extent that it would encourage fear of the sun, then in what shape is our environment? Wouldn't the authority of the AAP be better served by recommending that the US take decisive action to curb the spread of environmental pollution and perhaps even ratify the Kyoto Accord?

As usual, this is a one-size-fits-all recommendation even though everyone is not equally at risk. And watch for it to become a requirement within a few months. Somehow it is easier for the healthcare community to prescribe something to everyone rather than to educate those who are truly at risk or to take moral and ethical leadership in addressing the larger social problems implicit in its concerns.

Aside from the societal implications, as a parent I have a lot of specific questions about this recommendation, and unfortunately, these questions will not be seriously consid-

ered because this recommendation is already a fait accompli.
How many cases of rickets is this recommendation based
on? In which populations does rickets occur? Are there any
contributing causes to rickets other than lack of exposure to
sunlight? Were the babies who contracted rickets breastfed?
Were they exclusively breastfed? What are the risks and
benefits of supplementation with vitamin D? Have long-term
studies been done on the effects of vitamin D supplementation in infants? How long have the effects been tracked? Can
the benefits of sunlight really be put into a pill form? Does
synthetic sunlight have the same benefits as real sunlight?
What are the ingredients of the supplement? Are any genetically modified organisms included in the manufacture of
vitamin D? Is there a downside to convincing us all to fear
the sun? And, what if babies are given vitamin D and also go
out into the sun? Can they get too much vitamin D? Will we
hear 20 years from now about conditions related to vitamin
D toxicity? Will anyone be tracking this? What about other
countries, such as New Zealand and Australia, with higher
rates of skin cancer because of the hole in the ozone? What
are other pediatric organizations such as those in New Zealand, Australia, Canada, and Great Britain recommending in
this regard?

What about the economics of this recommendation?
How much will the vitamin D supplements cost? Will the 25
percent of parents who are poor have to pay for them? Who
will benefit from this recommendation? I understand that the
proposed vitamin D supplements are being produced by the
formula manufacturer Mead Johnson. One influential member
of the AAP recently expressed his hope that the formula
companies would stop manufacturing formula if they could
sell vitamin D. Does he imply a payback for the breastfeeding
recommendation? What percentage of the organization really
supports breastfeeding? What is the extent of the formula
companies' influence on the AAP? Is the vitamin D recommendation in any way related to the $8 million in renewable
grants to the AAP from the formula manufacturers or to
the $3 million donated by them for the AAP headquarters?
It would be hard for any organization, particularly one with

mixed loyalties, to resist this kind of financial pressure, and examples of similar special interest influence abound in our society. I'm especially distrustful when any official recommendation puts money into the pockets of the few by requiring the many to pay.

This recommendation is an example of how much normal life has become overmedicalized, fear-based, and viewed as pathology. I notice this trend in other areas as well. I recently saw an article describing several different breastfeeding "holds." Finally, I understood what I had been seeing for the last few years when I observed women breastfeeding in the most uncomfortable ways. In the 1970s, when I first breastfed, there were no different "holds." You just put the baby's head in the crook of your arm, brought her in close to the breast, made sure she was securely latched on, and sat back to enjoy breastfeeding. With many of these "holds," you can't sit back.

I noticed one coworker nursing her baby front-on, with the baby straddling her leg and holding onto the breast as if it were a bottle. The mom had to lean forward to sustain this position. I saw another old friend sitting with her baby lying in her lap, her one hand around the baby's back and head while another held her breast for him. Again, she had to lean over. And just recently I had breakfast with a friend who was attempting this same "hold" in an armless restaurant chair. Again, she had to lean forward. I couldn't stand it and had to ask her how she could possibly breastfeed this way. In my own experience, I could get comfortable only when I leaned back in the chair in which I was sitting. I can only imagine what my bodyworker friends would say if they saw these "holds," and I wondered how women could enjoy breastfeeding when they used them.

When I saw the article describing the different breastfeeding "holds" as though they were all created equal, I realized that women were actually being "taught" to breastfeed in these uncomfortable—and perhaps harmful—ways. These "holds," which were originally used for special circumstances—twins, cleft lip and palate, sucking difficulties—were now being recommended to everyone. The result, I think, is to overcomplicate breastfeeding. By teaching normal breastfeeding from the perspective of the few who encounter difficulties, fear is unnecessarily engendered, and a mother's inherent wisdom is once again undermined.

It is fear of another kind, fear of creeping medical fascism in the US, to which we respond. Nowhere is medical justice more trod upon than in the treatment of women who test positive for HIV and of their children. In our story, we bring you women like you and me. These are women with no symptoms of disease, no risk factors for AIDS, who by unfortunate circumstances tested positive—perhaps falsely—for HIV. Regardless of their past histories or status in society, these women were treated unjustly once they were identified as HIV-positive. These are the stories of women who've had the information and support to resist toxic treatments. Others have not been so lucky.

Like these women, we too must question authority. We can practice mental resistance, if that is the only alternative we have, to medical fascism. We can say no to the belief system that bullies and overpowers us into believing we're not in charge of our own lives. Mental resistance is the tactic of the 200,000 farmers in India who've been displaced by multinational agribusiness. It was the tactic of the Solidarity movement in Poland as well as the civil rights movement in this country. And mental resistance is the antidote to the tyranny of medical/pharmaceutical oppression.

We're not revolutionaries by choice. We are "just" parents, trying to do our best every day. Sometimes through no fault of our own, we get into circumstances that are oppressive. Other times, by just trying to do the right thing, we're subject to conflicting advice. Whether our lot in life is easy or difficult, we always find at the end of the day that no matter what the advice is or from whom it comes, we are ultimately the only ones who will live with the consequences of our own decisions.

If the official advice is not in keeping with your conscience this decade, wait a few years and it probably will be. Are you willing to wait for the medical dogma to catch up with you? Can you afford to? Lives hinge on your decisions. As mothers, we must find the higher power, the deeper way, by accessing the mystery that lives within us to solve the mysteries that life presents to us. It is in this way that we practice mental resistance against possible tyranny and thus ensure that our decisions as parents will be ethical, moral, and expressive of our personal integrity.

From Mothering, *issue no. 108 (September–October 2001).*

one world

As I write, it is just eight days after The Tragedy. Emotions are running high both inside of me and in the larger community, and I assume they still will be at the time of this reading. By the weekend after The Tragedy, I had lost all faith in my fellow humans. First, the terrible acts of destruction, then the vengeful talk of retaliation. For a while, we all went mad from the enormity of what had happened. This response is not unusual. Whenever we are wronged, we often first react with thoughts of revenge. Whether or not we act on these hateful thoughts is a test of our humanity.

In the family, just as in the world community, I have to choose every day to be adversarial or cooperative. And the more I choose cooperation, the more I must be willing to define, communicate, and enforce my own personal boundaries.

Early on in parenting, I chose cooperation. It wasn't easy. My first introduction to nonviolent discipline was the book *Liberated Parents, Liberated Children.* I felt totally out of control when I read the author's suggestion to abandon punishment. And I recognized, although it was painful, that what frightened me most about abandoning punishment was that I might not be able to have my own way.

As it turns out in the reality of the family, punishment is not actually a very effective tool for getting what we want. An adversarial relationship with our children often escalates or deteriorates as the child gets older because older, taller children are less intimidated by our threats. More importantly, the child who is punished—like our society that has been attacked—thinks not how wise her parents have been but about what she might do next to get back at them.

In the family, we learn a difficult truth that can provide a model for the current world conflict. Effective discipline is really based on our relationships with one another. Ultimately, it is our capacity for conscience and affection—not our fear of punishment—that prevents us from hurting one another.

As a new parent, I hit my children at first, and when I read *Liberated Parents* I decided to change. It took years. I first had the mental resolve but feared the loss of control. I didn't know what to do instead of spanking, and I wanted to postpone giving it up until I knew. At about that time, I saw a bumper sticker that read, "People Are Not for Hitting and Children Are People, Too." I realized then it was simply a decision. I didn't have to know what else to do. I just had to stop hitting and figure it out.

I discovered almost immediately that not hitting requires better boundaries. When I hit, I would wait until I got so angry that I blew up, thus justifying my actions. When I did not hit, I had to respond to the first stirrings of my anger so that I did not respond when my emotions or my actions were out of control. I came to realize that it is not the behavior of my children that creates my reactions, but rather my own inner resolve to parent nonviolently. If they act outrageously, this does not justify a violent response. It is not about their actions. It's all about my own inner resolve.

My inner resolve was born during the Vietnam War. I realized then, in my early 20s, that if I was serious about peace, I had to make peace with my family of origin. When I decided years later to have children and to raise them without punishment, it was these early yearnings for peace that spoke to me. I understood that the possibility of peace on earth begins with peace in the family. I wondered what society would be like if we could raise a whole generation of children nonviolently. What choices would those children make when they became our leaders? This is still my prayer and the work that you each do in your homes every day. Whether or not you are a pacifist and regardless of how you feel the US should respond to The Tragedy, I am sure that if

asked, you would say that you are raising your child nonviolently. I am sure that this is a value we all share.

So when the US media, politicians, and polls call for a violent response to The Tragedy, it is we not "they" I worry about.
This talk threatens members of our wonderful *Mothering* community. It threatens our international community of families. This
situation puts all of us at risk. In one instant, on that day, we
became one world. My community is no longer my neighborhood. In fact, I often have less contact with the people I live
near than with friends thousands of miles away. I cannot name
a potential "enemy country" that is not the home of a friend or
a friend of a friend or one of our readers.

Cynthia in Saudi Arabia is the moderator of the discussion boards at *www.mothering.com*. This week she e-mailed
me with concern over a mean-spirited thread on the boards.
At a time when our military threatened the region she lives
in, she was worried about my feelings. Our webmaster, Cynthia Marshall, was in London attending her mother's funeral
when The Tragedy happened. She told us of the fear in the
UK of an immediate retaliation by the US and her own fear
of being unable to get back home. Author Nitzan Gordon
e-mailed from Israel with kind words and letters of condolences from Palestinian mothers. They wanted us to know
that the images on the television of Palestinians celebrating
were not accurate. Photographer Lloyd Wolf sent photos
of people all over the world leaving offerings at US embas-
sies. Cynthia Good Mojab sent us an article about living in
two cultures. Her plea to not personalize The Tragedy and
harm Middle Eastern Americans was echoed by many. Just
yesterday I got a call from a Muslim American mother who
needed information on HIV and pregnancy. I was so happy
we could help her.

Contributor Wendy Ponte lost several firefighters in her
Brooklyn neighborhood, and her friend lost her husband.
The losses are beyond measure. And yet, military reprisal will
risk my beloved community. We have readers in more than
70 countries. I want to harm none of them. None of them is
disposable. There's no way that US military action will not
directly or indirectly hurt my friends. Like the workers in the

Twin Towers, the world is now too close not to share a common destiny. What happens to one of us could happen to any of us. Like the HIV-positive moms we profiled in the September–October issue, the vaccine-damaged children we reported on in the May–June issue, and welfare moms we bring you in this issue, we must understand that "there but for the grace of God go I."

In our families, if one of our children acts out violently, we will not rest until we understand the motivation for our child's behavior. Understanding is everything because once the behavior is understood, appropriate action can be taken, and the behavior is less likely to be repeated. Taking action to address our child's needs will make it unnecessary for him or her to use frustrated, angry outbursts to bring attention to problems. Seeking to understand does not imply that no action is taken but rather that the action will be proactive rather than reactive and will be based not only on an understanding of underlying motivations but also on a willingness for reconciliation.

Our behavior is orchestrated by the original melody of the early years of life. We are correct even at this time of common tragedy to redouble our efforts for peace in the family and peace in the world. Attending to the legitimate needs of our children and thereby raising children who have faith in their world will do more to heal the world than anything else.

So it is enough to go home and make peace with your family. Figure out how to do this. It will not be easy, so it will open your heart. Put family first in your life. Be political in whatever way you are inclined. Write a letter. Attend a meeting. Give a donation. But, most of all, speak up. Speak from your own feelings without blame or judgment. Don't bully others with your feelings, but speak up. Add your voice to the international conversation. Be inspired by the courage of Congresswoman Barbara Lee, who cast the lone vote in the House of Representatives against retaliation.

In 1988 we published an article by Thich Nhat Hanh entitled "Reconciliation." In this article, he describes seven practices of conflict resolution and reconciliation that have evolved in Buddhist monasteries over the last 2,500 years. First is Face-to-Face Sitting, in which the entire community sits together mindfully, breathing, with the willingness to help and not to fight.

The second practice is Remembrance, in which the two monks in conflict try to remember the whole history of the conflict, every detail of the conflict, while the community just sits patiently and listens.

The third practice is Non-stubbornness. Everyone in the community expects the two monks not to be stubborn. The outcome is less important than the fact that each monk is doing his best to show a willingness for reconciliation and understanding.

The fourth practice is Covering Mud with Straw. One respected senior monk is appointed to represent each side of the conflict and to say things about "his" monk that will help the other better understand and de-escalate his feelings, his anger, and his resistance.

Next is Voluntary Confession. Each monk reveals his own shortcomings without waiting for others to state them. The atmosphere of the community is supportive, expecting that the de-escalation will be realized. The senior monk reminds the monks to think of the larger community and its well-being.

Lastly are the Decision by Consensus and Accepting the Verdict. It is agreed in advance that the two monks will accept the decision of the whole group or leave the community. The decision involves suggested actions for each monk, and the entire community is asked three times if it accepts the verdict.

This process reminds me of something I stumbled on by accident with my children. When there was a conflict (and there were a lot), I would take the two involved aside and listen intently to each side of the story, one at a time with the other present. I was surprised to find that once they both had spoken, they each spontaneously jumped up and ran off to play again. They just needed to be heard.

If The Tragedy were about my kids, I would say, "No more hitting. Keep talking. Keep interacting." The Tragedy is, of course, bigger than my family, bigger than the US. It affects the world community, and yet the principles are the same. Armed retaliation will hurt the family and friends of our international community of mothers. And it will hurt the families here in the US whose children will be called to fight. There can be no winners.

Since the world leaders are having trouble figuring out what to do to resolve the conflicts in the Middle East, perhaps we should volunteer our expertise as mothers. In all countries, we could form groups of mothers—International Mothers for Peace—that would be willing to hear both sides of the story and make a consensus decision. This process is something mothers are particularly skilled at; we do it every day. We could start right away.

Mothering got a letter this week from Karen: "I am writing to ask you to help guide us pacifist mothers in how to prevent the US from systematically terrorizing families in other countries as a retaliation for Tuesday's events." Karen, this poem's for you.

From Mothering, *issue no. 109 (November–December 2001).*

your children mine

Aren't you tired of it?
Aren't you just tired of it?
Seeing those faces
In helmets and uniforms
Carrying rifles.
Seeing those young faces in the newspaper.
Black faces.
Brown faces.
Red faces.
White faces.
Yellow faces.
Young faces.
Wearing the grim look of war.
Doing the dirty work of their grown-up puppeteers
Who condemn to die each year
Thousands, millions of our newest souls
Because we haven't learned how to talk to
one another.
To negotiate with honor.
To compromise with power.
To value human life.
So we take the easy way out.
The easy way of violence.
The lazy way of killing.
The whole symbolic transference of power
From old to young
Done on the battlefield of death.
But the power passes.
The old die
And the young remember.
The young who've had to fight at others' bidding,
The young who've seen their buddies die.
We must some soon decade
STOP
The Sacrificing
Of the young
For false and temporary
Glory.

having a baby in america

FOR MORE THAN TWENTY YEARS, I have listened to
women talk about their intentions before birth and have been
fascinated to compare this talk to what they report afterward.
Often, as new mothers, we are disappointed when things do
not turn out as we had hoped and planned. We are confused
and blame ourselves. We wonder what might have been different about our baby's birth and what simply must be accepted.
What does a woman require to birth normally? What are the
qualities and experiences that allow a woman to have the confidence necessary to believe in her capacity to birth normally?

We now know many things that contribute to this confidence, but most women in the US do not yet receive them.
For those who do—who birth with a midwife or have a supporting doula—pregnancy is an opportunity for empowerment and maturation. Pregnancy and birth, in fact, are by
nature transformative. Despite our best efforts to rid ourselves
of our conditioning in the US, we are still subject, unfortunately, to the beliefs of our culture about the limited capacity
of women. We must expand our sense of ourselves in order to
birth normally. We must radicalize ourselves.

The beauty industry, fashion industry, and drug industry
all tell us the same thing. We are not good enough as we are.
We need something more. The birth industry suggests, by its
very existence, that we are not equal to birth, and it implies
that we will need drugs or interventions. These doubts about
our capacity to birth normally are deep and pervasive, rooted
in our fear of death, our lack of comfort with the intimate, and

our suspicion of the feminine. Bringing consciousness to these things as pregnant women makes our birth choices much more than lifestyle choices. In this light, birth becomes, in fact, a political act.

Having a baby in America is a political act because to birth normally you must keep your vision of your own inherent capacity strongly in focus to resist the competing special interests that vie for dominance of your birth experience. American insurance companies define pregnancy as a disability; obstetrical medicine practices defensively to ward off malpractice suits; pharmaceutical companies and manufacturers of birth technology offer incentives to practitioners to try their products; in short, birth has become a business. While we hope as pregnant women that our needs will be put first, we are often overpowered by the culture of medicalized birth.

As pregnant and birthing women, we are naturally vulnerable and might rightly assume that our vulnerability would be appreciated by society and that we would feel protected. Unfortunately, this is not always the case in the US, where so many families live in poverty and many women simply cannot afford prenatal care. This is so in 2002 despite the fact that the National Commission to Prevent Infant Mortality called for access to prenatal care for all women as long ago as 1988. Even when a woman can afford health insurance, her policy may not give her any real choice regarding birth.

We have a lending library for the local community in Santa Fe, and a woman came into our office recently to check out some books. She recounted how she had been refused an appointment at the local medical practice she had been previously using because she had gone up to Taos to see the birth center there. She was told by the local practice that she had fired them by consulting another practice. This dumbfounded her, as she was newly pregnant and had just moved back to the area. She had legitimate concerns about her previous births that made her want to explore various options. However, she was severely censured for simply getting more information and for doing so openly.

We wrote in issue 109 about a couple who were also censured, but in a different way, for bringing a birth plan to the hospital. The medical profession carries a difficult burden, to be sure. We expect physicians to do everything right to save our lives, and yet we are often too eager to blame them when things go wrong. It is difficult as new parents, however, to break away from the contemporary adversarial quality of health care. This is what makes it imperative that you find a compatible birth attendant regardless of the cost. If this is simply impossible, it is essential that you at least have a birth advocate, labor coach, or doula with you at all times during labor. These things are not simply good ideas. They can make the difference between whether you feel victimized or power-ful after birth. They may even affect whether you begin life as a new family traumatized or ecstatic.

Why is it necessary to have someone with you at all times? Why am I making such a big deal of this? I'm alarmed. I have been working to advocate natural childbirth for nearly 30 years, and things are getting worse. Women are at risk, regardless of their inclination toward natural birth. Pregnancy and birth interventions, surgical birth, and maternal death are all on the increase in US hospitals. Tragically, as women birthing in these hospitals, we are at risk of being subjected to machines, procedures, and surgeries that are used routinely and yet are simply not supported by evidence.

And what is worse, we have accepted this situation as normal. Women in the US actually believe that we need these things. More than one-third of us give birth surgically. More than 40 percent use drugs during birth, even though we spend our pregnancies avoiding them. We are at the mercy of an insa-tiable medical technology, one that will offer us more and more technology until we simply refuse. Mothers, where do you stand on this? How can we regain our power as birthing women? How can we believe again in our capacity to birth normally?

In the 1970s, when birth practices changed dramatically in the US and more options began to be available to families, there were powerful groups of parents who worked with mid-wives for legislation and social acceptance. These were often people who had been inspired by their baby's birth experience to believe in their own inherent integrity. It is a time now for such people and such groups to rise up again. We must organize together in our communities to encourage natural birth and to build a supportive subculture of normal birth, a "village" within each of our towns.

The cesarean rate in 1960 in the US was 7 percent. Today, despite the World Health Organization's recommendation of a 10 to 12 percent cesarean rate, the US rate is over 20 percent and on the rise. Now, you tell me, were women's bodies different in 1960? Are women's bodies different in other countries? Of course not! The increased rate is related to a recent decline in the number of vaginal births after cesareans (VBAC) due to lack of medical encouragement. Remember that your birth will be impacted by its cultural and social milieu as well as by your own personal psychology. So you must make your birth a political act if you are to ensure that it is evidence-based rather than driven by special interests.

As if the high rate of forceps, vacuum extraction, and cesarean section were not enough, you can also count on the use of experimental drugs in US hospitals and among some US midwives. In issue 107, we published an article on the dangers of Cytotec, a peptic ulcer drug that is used off-label for labor induction and that is so powerful it can cause uterine rupture and even death. It is the use of this drug for induction in women with previous cesareans that has recently given VBACs a bad name. It's not the VBAC. They're perfectly safe. It's the drug that is unsafe.

If you are offered drugs during birth, don't be naive. Ask questions. You asked about everything you put into your body while you were pregnant. Don't stop while you're giving birth. Ask about the drugs, or tell your doula to do so.

But why do we take drugs anyway? Usually we do not have the support we need to explore nondrug soothers or our natural chemistry for relief. We seldom have the opportunity to consider the effects of the drugs on the baby beforehand. We may mistakenly think of birth pain as a nuisance, something that should be eliminated because it can be. The experience of normal birth, however, is intangible.

In 1982 psychiatrist Ronald Laing wrote, "We do not see childbirth in many obstetric units now. What we see resembles childbirth as much as artificial insemination resembles sexual intercourse. And birth, as a home and family event, has virtually been cultured out. Women are allowed or not to have their babies at home. In hospitals, they are allowed or not to move, scream or sing, stand, walk, sit or squat. Women are allowed or not to have their babies after birth. To allow is to exercise as much, if not more power, than to forbid." Laing pleaded for genuine choice, asking, "Why should any one way have to be imposed on all? Why cannot two or more ways coexist in the same society? Why should there be any monopoly on what is available?"

As members of the animal kingdom, we have a beautiful, inherently elegant, and precise physiological blueprint for birth that is often undermined and seldom acknowledged by the habits and common practices of US hospitals. Such institutions change slowly, and their policies are often based on economies of efficiency rather than emotional well-being.

Emotional well-being, however, is precisely what we must ensure. It is our responsibility to protect our unborn baby and ourselves from unhealthy environments. To do so, we need to become radicalized. We must put aside the limited view that others have of our potential and our capacity, rely on the generations who have successfully birthed before us, and generate a new and broader vision of ourselves as birthing women. We must be like my friend Elizabeth, who replied when her mother called her a "poor thing" during her labor, "I'm not a poor thing. I'm a warrior."

Where is your warrior? Where is your wild side? Where does the animal live in you? For it is the animal in you who will give birth. In the 1970s, we felt liberated because women had increased opportunities in the workplace, yet we were still washing all the dishes. We are not yet liberated in our lives today if we are not in charge of our own birth experiences. Today, we must see that liberation in the workplace is only the beginning. We must reject the passivity that allows us to accept without question health care that is often experimental.

The president of the American College of Obstetricians and Gynecologists publicly recommends elective cesareans rather than vaginal births. To suggest to US women that surgery is equal to vaginal birth is the ultimate deception.

How gullible are we? A cesarean is surgery. Sarah Buckley's article in this issue dramatically illustrates how nature has elegantly provided us with an ecstatic hormonal chemistry designed to comfort us during birth, keep our baby alert after birth, and prepare us for bonding and breastfeeding. It is this delicate and essential chemistry that we miss when our births are orchestrated by medical technology.

We holler about choice as though all choices were created equal. What choices are truly important? Perhaps the most important is first to decide where you want to give birth. Then choose a practitioner with whom you are compatible, one who sees birth as normal and who does not interfere with nature.

Real choice is not about accepting the limited options offered you by insurance companies and conservative medicine in one country at one time in the history of the world. Real choice requires thinking out of the box. It means recognizing the fact that you are a parent as soon as you become pregnant and that it is never too soon to begin to take responsibility for your baby and your future life together. It is also never too late to find a new birth attendant. Nature has provided you and your baby with instinctual aids intrinsic to the pregnancy and birth experience. Rely on them. They make things much easier, and not surprisingly they also facilitate your future life together.

On the other hand, when you choose the medical model for birth, things are more difficult. Interventions lead to other interventions. You are continually questioning yourself. Does starting out life as a new mother with birth interventions make us more likely to need intervention at future parental transitions? Does this process make us more likely to trust experts and less likely to trust ourselves?

As parents, our expertise is inherent. We must step back from the limited view ascribed to women and mothers by modern-day US culture and uncover a deeper, more primitive confidence in ourselves. Let the animal in you out. Listen to her. Let her lead. Once you get to know her, you'll recognize her. She is the part of you that is always on your side.

From Mothering, *issue no. 111 (March–April 2002).*

tv is not good for kids

LAST SUNDAY I WAS IN THE BALTIMORE AIRPORT on
my way home from DC. As I walked through the airport, the
obscene cover headline of *Newsweek* magazine jumped out at
me from every newsstand: TV Is Good for Kids. Perhaps no
article before has so sadly illustrated the extent of the decline
of independent news reporting in the US. November 11, 2002,
will go down in infamy as the day journalism died. What's
especially tragic is that millions will believe the headline without reading the article, and those who read the article may
believe what it says. It is superbly crafted to dismiss or omit
contrary views. While it has always been true that journalism
is opinion, not fact, it is now painfully obvious that opinion
is for sale.

The article fails to mention that *Newsweek* is owned by
the *Washington Post,* which also owns six television stations:
WDIV in Detroit, KPRC in Houston, WPLG in Miami, WKMP
in Orlando, KSAT in San Antonio, and WJXT in Jacksonville
as well as a regional cable system. It's telling that this article
appears during an economic slump in which print advertising
is down across the industry. On its website, the *Washington
Post* states that it hopes to offset this slump in print advertising by boosting profits with cable revenues. Certainly this
article will help. The two media companies mentioned most
in the article, Nickelodeon and Disney, are cable channels.

The author also fails to disclose that the primary expert
cited in the article, Daniel Anderson, PhD, of the University
of Massachusetts, works as a paid consultant to industry and

advertising. His clients include NBC, CBS, Universal Pictures, Sony, General Mills, the Leo Burnett ad agency, Nickelodeon, and the National Association of Broadcasters. And it is not clear in the article if the studies mentioned are independently or industry funded. The research that shows that children learn from television simply confirms what we already know about TV. Children do learn from it, and much of what they learn is harmful. To leave out all other research— research that has been unanimous in documenting TV's deleterious effects—and to assert that TV is good for kids because one programming study showed that children learn from it, is highly unethical. What is particularly unethical is that this article is about toddlers, children under three. The photo accompanying the article shows toddlers, and the article extols the benefits of TV for this age group.

The American Academy of Pediatrics (AAP) is very concerned about the language and developmental impact of television programming intended for children younger than two and adamantly opposes programming and marketing to children this young. The academy confirms that TV can limit more important interactions with parents, other adults, and children as well as encourage passive rather than active communications such as reading, listening to music, and playing, all of which are paramount to a child's normal development.

Specifically, the AAP said, "Pediatricians should urge parents to avoid television viewing for children under the age of two years. Although certain television programs may be promoted to this age group, research on early brain development shows that babies and toddlers have a critical need for direct interactions with parents and other significant caregivers for healthy brain growth and the development of appropriate social, emotional, and cognitive skills. Therefore, exposing such young children to television programs should be discouraged."

For children older than two, the AAP recommends that total TV consumption be limited to one to two hours a day and that such programming should be developmentally based, prosocial, and nonviolent and should reinforce language and social skills. The average television consumption by children is

3 hours a day, or 21 hours a week. This is about 20 percent of
a child's waking day and does not include time spent playing
and watching video games and movies.

It's not just the programming, however, that is of concern
for parents. Advertising is the bigger culprit. By the time a
child has graduated from high school, she will have viewed
360,000 advertisements. The AAP states that advertising
directed toward children is inherently deceptive and exploits
children under eight years of age "because children who are
developmentally younger than 8 are unable to understand the
intent of advertisements and, in fact, accept advertising claims
as true."

One of the advertising claims that little girls accept as fact
is that thin is beautiful. Thirty-one percent of nine-year-old
girls think they are too fat, and 11 percent of eighth-grade girls
are on diets. The Kaiser Family Foundation recently found that
teenage girls, most of whom watch 20 hours of TV a week,
are bombarded by images of extremely thin women (e.g.,
Ally McBeal). While the average American woman is about
five feet, four inches tall and weighs 142 pounds, the average
model is five feet, nine inches tall and weighs 110 pounds. At
least 15 percent of Miss America contestants are underweight.

Conversely, TV is also implicated in obesity because it is
the principal cause of inactivity in kids and adults. Twenty-
five percent of children are overweight, and the number of
overweight children ages 6 to 17 has doubled since 1968.
Between 1982 and 1994, cases of type 2 diabetes, the type of
diabetes most closely linked to weight, quadrupled among
kids. Adult obesity usually begins in childhood. In 1999 the
Journal of the American Medical Association called obesity an
epidemic. Its occurrence has increased by 25 percent during
the last 30 years, and between 1991 and 1998, there was an
increase in obesity in all states, both sexes, all ages, and all
socioeconomic groups.

In addition to unreal images of feminine beauty and advertisements for junk food, the average young viewer is exposed
to 14,000 sexual references each year. Only a handful of these
provide an accurate portrayal of responsible sexual behavior
or accurate information about birth control, abstinence, or

the risks of pregnancy and transmitting sexual diseases.

As if the risk of obesity and diabetes and the incidences of anorexia and bulimia are not enough bad news for our children, the studies on television and violence confirm the toxicity. More than 1,000 scientific studies and reviews have concluded that significant exposure to media violence increases the risk of aggressive behavior in certain children and adolescents, desensitizes them to violence, and makes them believe that the world is a mean and dangerous place. In addition, news reports of bombings, natural disasters, murders, and other violent crimes can potentially traumatize young children.

The March 29, 2002, edition of *Science* published the latest in articles that document an association between television viewing and violence. "Television Viewing and Aggressive Behavior During Adolescence and Adulthood" reported on a study involving 700 young people over a 16-year period. Of youths who watched less than an hour of TV a day at age 14, just 5.7 percent were involved in aggressive acts by ages 16 to 22, as compared with 22.5 percent of those who watched one to three hours a day and 45.2 percent of males and 12.7 percent of females who watched more than three hours a day. These aggressive acts took the form of threats to injure, general aggressive acts, physical fights, assaults, robberies, and the use of weapons to commit crimes.

Some experts predict that as much as 25 to 50 percent of the anger and violence in our society is due to the culture of violence that has been created by the television and film industries and is reinforced on a daily basis. Dr. David Pearl, chief of behavioral science at the National Institute of Mental Health, reports a causal link between viewing TV violence and subsequent aggressive behavior. He cites a 22-year New York study that found "the best single prediction of aggressiveness at 19 years of age turned out to be the TV programs the subjects preferred when they were 8 years old at the beginning of the study." Those with the heaviest diets of violent entertainment as children were convicted of criminal offenses 150 percent more often than those from the same classrooms with the lightest diets of violent entertainment as children. Former

US surgeon general David Satcher stated in a 2000 report on youth violence that violent television programming and video games are a public health issue and that "repeated exposure to violent entertainment during early childhood causes more aggressive behavior throughout a child's life."

The American Psychological Association (APA) notes that children who regularly watch violence on television are more fearful and distrustful of the world, less bothered by violence, and slower to intervene or call for help when they see fighting or destructive behavior. A poll by the *Los Angeles Times* reported that 91 percent of children said they felt "upset" or "scared" by violence on television. A University of Pennsylvania study found that children's TV shows contain roughly 20 acts of violence each hour. After watching violent programs, the APA reports, children are more likely to act out aggressively, and children who are regularly exposed to violent programming show a greater tendency toward hitting, arguing, leaving tasks unfinished, and impatience.

The Yale University Family Television and Consultation Center reveals that imagination decreases as TV watching increases. Complex language and grammar skills are directly linked to fantasy play, and children who create fantasy play are more tolerant, peaceful, patient, and happy. I recall that my own children's play was more imaginative when they didn't watch television.

Joseph Chilton Pearce, author of *Magical Child* and, most recently, *The Biology of Transcendence,* says that it is television itself, not only its programming, that is dangerous. He says that children need the early time of imagination and play and that watching television prematurely matures their brains for more abstract thinking.

The 60-year research of Paul MacLean, former director of the Laboratory of Brain Evolution and Behavior at the National Institute of Mental Health, shows that we are never a mindless body. We are always using all three of our brains—reptilian: physical survival; limbic: group survival; and neocortex: survival of our creations. Information from the outside world goes first to the reptilian brain and then to the neocortex. All three brains perceive an image. The first and

second brain, by their nature, believe and accept the image
as true. A half second elapses and hundreds of thousands of
nerve relationships occur between the time the reptile in us
senses something and the human in us classifies it. By the
time that happens, we will have already had a physical and
emotional experience.

Therefore, when our children watch heightened, even
disturbing events on television, even when they watch animal
shows, their nervous systems will register what they see as real
for half a second. Television will keep them, in a number of
cases, in a constant state of arousal, even elicit a fight-or-flight
hormonal response. It's not until the television is off that the
images are digested. Many parents report that their children
are overly active following television viewing. The inactivity
and the hormonal stimulation of the television might neces-
sitate physical activity to help integrate the experience.

It is clearly untrue to say that TV is good for kids. While
educational programming may be increasing, many of these
efforts are designed to capture an audience of children under
age three, despite the objections of parents, physicians, and
psychologists. While the article reports that people educated
in child psychology act as consultants to television shows, it is
not clear whom they work for and whether their recommendations will be used for programming or market research. It's
clear, however, that our babies are being studied in order to
learn how to better captivate them.

The article further touted a study that demonstrates
that children learn from TV. This is not new information
and only adds to what we already know. It should make us
cautious, however, not celebratory. It is irresponsible for the
article to recommend television for those under three and
for the cover headline to so grossly overstate the evidence.
Why would a magazine like *Newsweek* stoop to such deceptive journalism?

Other research that was cited in this article must scare the
television industry. Twenty-two percent of parents consider
getting rid of television altogether, and 93 percent think the
"right" TV shows are OK in moderation. Clearly, these numbers mean that the market of television viewers is declining.

Similar combinations of sensational headlines, faulty research, and questionable experts occur by design over and over again to protect industry, even the medical industry. We report in this issue on the all-too-familiar shenanigans of the throwaway-diaper industry, which cost us the cloth-diaper industry in the 1990s. And just this last year, I've seen this same combination used to attack free choice in parenting. Vaginal births, vaginal births after cesareans, homebirth, cosleeping, and breastfeeding have all been threatened by poor studies and bad press at the same time that elective cesareans, vaccinations with mercury preservatives, and television have been extolled as safe, even good for us. In all cases, the studies (usually one) on which these new fears are promulgated have been widely criticized for faulty data, and yet the public may have already gotten the wrong idea. Tragically, media monopolies have made journalism unreliable.

What this *Newsweek* article illustrates is that the media concentration of the last ten years has created an inherent conflict of interest for many publishers. The interests of advertisers have taken precedence over the interests of readers. What we need now is policy that works to change this media concentration by enforcing antitrust regulations. The best description of the current media dilemma can be found in the book *Rich Media, Poor Democracy,* by Robert McChesney. Television is the principal way that advertisers access our children. When we limit our children's access to television, we also limit corporate predators' access to our children. Limiting television viewing is the single best thing you can do to protect your children from the influences of commercialism. To help educate yourself about the effects of television, check out these two websites: *www.commercial alert.org* and *www.turnofftv.org.*

From Mothering, *issue no. 116 (January–February 2003).*

drilling for hope

DURING TIMES IN OUR LIVES when we feel oppressed or dominated by others, it can be difficult to remain hopeful or to feel powerful. The early days and weeks of motherhood are one of those times. We love the baby madly, but we mourn the loss of control over our own lives. To regain a semblance of control, we learn new attitudes and habits for tough times.

Today's political climate is another kind of tough time. Regardless of our political stance on the issues, we all feel dominated by a world situation that we cannot control. While we don't want to bury our heads in the sand and pretend that nothing is happening, neither do we want to be victimized by the propaganda that tells us we are powerless. And, most important, we must remain optimistic for our children.

Optimism is a characteristic that is inculcated in the human spirit during the first five years of life and one that we reinforce every day as parents. We must be living examples of optimism and sow optimism in the spirits of our children. Cynicism will find its way to them soon enough. Optimism is at the core of our ability to survive.

This is a very exciting time, history in the making. New ways are being born in the world; old ways are dramatically dying. I find that I must choose between recognizing the evidence of a new society or being seduced by the propaganda of the old.

One piece of evidence is the huge antiwar rallies and demonstrations of the last few months. At the same time that the old world order of control and dominance is ever more determined, a new world ethic of peace, cooperation, and personal authority is longing to be born. Citizens are no longer willing to accept the voice of authority absent of evidence. Evidence is authority. In all institutions and in every arena of life, we see a scrambling to maintain order and to enforce arbitrary authority, a tendency to convince on the basis of fear rather than trust.

It is essential, however, to hunt for a point of view that is based on trust and that keeps you optimistic. Fight the necessary inner battles to maintain that point of view. Counter the propaganda that encourages you to consider yourself ever the terrified victim kept off balance by fear of the unknown. Insist on balance. Trust the unknown. Develop strategies that help you maintain your own separate reality, a strong personal belief system that supports optimism and keeps you connected to others.

Here are suggestions for maintaining helpful attitudes and mental habits in tough times:

Choose your sources of information carefully. In the same way that you must look for alternative news about parenting if you want to have the whole, unbiased story, so do you have to look for alternative sources of news and information. Television news is more entertainment than news. *USA Today* and most local newspapers are advertising vehicles and, therefore, are seldom controversial. They are poor choices for unbiased coverage. Voices opposed to war are not often heard, and the human costs of war are simply not discussed. The good news is that there are varied news sources on the Internet, and international websites like *www.independent.co.uk* present a broader view.

Beware of psychic pollution. Learn how to put news in its proper perspective. Many of us are suffering from information overload and can become addicted to dramatic news with its life-or-death pitch. This is a manufactured reality, a heightened reality like a drug or alcohol high. We can become addicted to the drama. Limit your digestion of sensational news. Don't allow your thoughts to become dominated by the lives of strangers and events you cannot control. Be ruthless about what you allow into your mind. Make an agreement with yourself about how much time you will worry about a given subject each day. Stick to it. You will notice a difference in how you feel. Be especially vigilant about the psychic pollution of children. Protect them fiercely from cynicism and from overexposure to the adult world.

Make your world smaller. The domination of media and advertising can overpower our personal lives with a bigger, more fearful world. We have to choose which world holds our allegiance. If we really look around our own lives, in our own towns and our neighborhoods, we see that things are not as fearful or violent as they are often portrayed in the media. We have to trust the reality of our own lives, of our own neighborhoods. Get close to your world. Go out walking in the woods near your house or in your neighborhood. Get to know your immediate environment by getting to know your neighbors and spending more time at home. You will find that a comforting reality exists all around you.

Grow a progressive community. When we feel oppressed by circumstances or by society, it is often because we feel alone. It's important in tough times to find a community of like-minded people. In the early years as parents, questions about our children bring us together, and these early communities can sustain us through our whole parenting lives. We can also develop communities of people who share our same political, social, environmental, or spiritual beliefs. Invite a group of mothers over regularly for food and conversation. Talk while the children play.

Take solace in the ordinary. It is the everyday occurrences of life that sustain us. Infuse everyday events with magic and ritual. Make meals a time of community and connection with loved ones. Eat at home more. Ask friends over for dinner. Turn washing, drying, and ironing clothes into acts that add order and rhythm to life. Rediscover the smell of line-dried clothes. Make your home a place of solace and refuge. Create an inspiring and regenerative personal environment. You will feel a difference.

Sing and dance. In the most difficult of times, people sing and dance. Get some new music to listen to in the car or at home. Better yet, get together with friends to listen to and play live music. Sing together at holidays and anytime people get together. Teach yourself songs in the shower and the car. And dance anywhere. Dance to music in the living room, in the car, while you're gardening or working outside. Immerse yourself in music, and it will make you feel better.

Choose your companions carefully. In times of oppression and difficulties, it is especially important to keep good companions. Our companions strongly influence not only our opinion of ourselves but also our state of mind. The victimized, dramatic emotions of others can influence us to develop a more negative and hopeless view of the world. On the other hand, companions who have a new sense of things or who talk of life in positive and hopeful terms can help us feel strong enough to tackle life's challenges. These friends give us courage.

Lead an examined life. Tough times require honesty and self-reflection, because it is easy to take things personally during tough times. Increased self-awareness allows us to take responsibility appropriately and to let go of what we can't control. It is important to cultivate the habit of self-reflection.

Focus your attention outside of yourself. Sometimes when we are absorbed by a problem in our family or in society at large, we lose all perspective. We think that our situation or our time is the worst in the history of the world. We exaggerate our own importance. Serving others, especially children, can put things in perspective.

Become an activist. When you have a child, you realize that being a parent is the most important activism you will ever do. Yet in these times of social upheaval, we have a duty to do more. Find a cause that you believe in and support it at whatever level you can. Give money or time. Become a member. Educate and organize others. Vote. Register others to vote. And remember that activism is not about instant success but about social change in the long haul. It takes time.

Talk to your kids about peace. While others may wonder how to talk to children about war, talk to your children about peace. Protect them from overexposure to war talk and war images. It's important to answer their questions openly and honestly, but follow their lead. Include them in conversations

about peace and justice. Talk openly with them and others
about your beliefs.

Don't be a victim. So much media propaganda leaves us
feeling terrified and helpless. Any time you feel helpless, gather
together your thoughts and your resources. Spend more time
with like-minded people to feel more powerful. And don't be
afraid to change. Do what you need to in order to remain optimistic. You'll feel more in control of your life if you act on your
beliefs.

Start with yourself. If you are unhappy with society and
wish that it were different, make the changes in yourself that
you would like to see in others. Get to know yourself better.
If you wish that others were less mean-spirited, become so
yourself. If you long for compassion and empathy, practice these
qualities with those you disapprove of. Act democratically. Let
change begin with you.

Don't turn against yourself in tough times. Often, when
times are hard, we bemoan our bad luck. Why me? Why now?
When you can refrain from taking life personally, however,
you can act more effectively. Tough times will generate courage in proportion to the difficulty of the situation.

Imagine it into becoming. It is tempting to criticize
things as they are without having any idea of how to improve
them. Part of the seduction of modern times is the false belief
that this is as good as it gets, that things couldn't possibly
be any better. The wisdom of living your own reality despite
tough times is that your everyday reality ever improves itself;
it always gives birth to a more positive future. Spend time
imagining solutions to the problems you face in your life or
to the problems of society. Talk to your friends about positive
solutions. Take action to add at least one positive solution to
your life.

Keep your sense of humor. At the heart of an optimistic
spirit is a hearty sense of humor. When you can laugh at yourself and the world, you can keep perspective. When you can't,
you know that you need some help. Suffering happens, but
it can be borne more easily with a loving heart. Reach out to
others when you've lost your sense of humor. Watch a funny
movie or do the Twist.

It is a loving heart and an optimistic spirit that are required
now. In the 1960s, many disillusioned young people dropped
out of society and went "back to the land." Even though we had
stopped a war and retired a president, we did not realize our
political power and had no idea how to sustain it. It's different
now. We must create our own personal realities to raise our
children with hope and optimism, but not drop out. We must
become increasingly active in re-creating democracy in our
lives and in our society. Our personal lives parallel the collective. Speak with your own voice, and it will uplift others. Work
on your own life, and it will inspire others. Come together
with one another, and you will touch others. Keep hope alive
for the future, for the children. Children are the evidence that
love, not fear, is the answer.

From Mothering, *issue no. 118 (May–June 2003).*

gathering the mothers

MOTHERING MAGAZINE WAS STARTED IN 1976 to celebrate mothers. The 1970s were a critical time in history, when the roles of women were being redefined and when mothers were increasingly entering the workforce. At that time, feminism in the US was focused on equal rights for women, not on the politics of motherhood, and many women got the message that it was not good enough to be "just" a mom. By the 1980s, the proverbial dinner-party question, "And what do you do?" had become such a cliché that creative moms at home made up such titles as "social engineer" to use as clever retorts. Clearly, women were at odds with each other over their choices.

By the 1990s, the new world of female economic opportunity was beginning to crack around the edges. Once women no longer had to fight for access to a "man's world," they realized that it wasn't all it was cracked up to be. There was the glass ceiling, the unequal pay, and while feminine qualities of leadership transformed the work world, they did so often at a cost to personal life.

Women found, just as men had before them, that work isn't everything. They began to question the pursuit of materialism and started to give themselves permission to stay home again and to make creative work arrangements. The irregularities of daycare and nannies raised new questions. While the numbers of working moms continued to rise well into the eighties and early nineties, by the late nineties and

the new century, the numbers had begun to level off and
even decline.

By the new century, mothers were less likely to be defensive
about their choices and more likely to recognize the low social
status of mothers as the source of their common oppression.
Improving the social status of mothers is what many of the
organizations listed here want to do. We desperately need
to recognize the value of mothers, and no one should ever
have to apologize again for being "just a mom." In fact, it's a
whole new world for moms today, a veritable renaissance for
mothers. Many of the organizations, centers, and offerings I've
envisioned for moms are coming to fruition.

Several times over the last few years, I've visited the
Waldorf community in Fair Oaks, California, and have long
admired the Mothers' Support Network (*www.motherssup-
portnetwork.org*), started there in 1992 by Marianne Alsop
and Barbara Daly. Their mission is "to support parents in their
quest to raise happy, healthy children." They have regular support meetings, scheduled play days, a mother-baby program,
childbirth preparation classes, parent-toddler classes, community events, a library, and a newsletter.

Marianne, Barbara, and I have talked often about how we
want to see this type of support network in every community, and their work provides a model. There is nothing like
mother-to-mother, home-to-home support. It is important
that parents get information and support directly from other
parents in informal settings. Meetings in homes are sufficient,
or the network may eventually grow into a center, just as is
happening in Fair Oaks. If you want to start a group or a center, there are three organizations, in addition to the Mothers'
Support Network, that can help you. The National Association
of Mothers' Centers (NAMC; *www.motherscenter.org*) will help
you find or start a mothers' center in your area. Its mission is
"to enable members to be effective in using their individual
and collective knowledge and experience as catalysts for personal and societal changes that benefit mothers and families."
NAMC wants to break the isolation of mothers, to advance
our healing and well-being, and to recognize the importance
of mothers to society, both their paid and unpaid work.

While neither NAMC nor the International Moms Clubs (*www.momsclub.org*) advocate a particular philosophy, the Moms Clubs are particularly for at-home moms. The organization's goals are "to provide a support group for mothers who choose to stay at home to raise their children." Further, it wants to "provide a forum for topics of interest to mothers," to help children in the community, and to perform community service.

Another group especially for moms at home is Mothers of Color at Home (MOCHA; *www.mochamoms.org*). The group is a "support group for mothers of color who have chosen not to work full time outside of the home in order to devote more time to their families." The group is accepting new members and organizing new chapters in areas with several members.

Another new group is working for the inclusion of the voices of mothers in the public conversation. The Motherhood Project, founded by Enola Aird in 2000, is working to promote "a Mother's Renaissance—fresh thinking, discussion and activism by mothers about motherhood and mothering, and about who mothers are, what we do, our importance to our children, families and society, and our potential as catalysts for cultural and social change for the benefit of children and families."

When I first talked to Enola Aird of the Motherhood Project several years ago, I knew at once that we shared a kindred passion for the subject of mothering and that we both wanted social change in the US. The Motherhood Project has issued two statements. Issued in May 2001, "Watch Out for Children: A Mothers' Statement to Advertisers" (*www.watchoutforchildren.org*) warns of the catastrophic effects of commercialism on children. The second, "Call to a Motherhood Movement," November 2002, was first presented at a symposium on maternal feminism at Barnard College on October 29, 2002.

I am a member of the Mothers' Council of the Motherhood Project, where I serve with a diverse group of women who defy the labels of "liberal" or "conservative." Over the issues of family, I find myself aligned with people and organizations with whom I do not agree 100 percent. I do not require it. I'm proud to add my name, for example, to appeals and initiatives also signed by Phyllis Schlafly. I'm eager to join together with her and others who want to curb the spread of commercialism and support decent public policy for families. I would love to see us put down the past divisions of the feminist movement, the mommy wars and partisan politics, and join together as grown-up women to further causes that help mothers and children of all classes and colors.

Last fall, Enola invited me to join her and some other motherhood leaders at a dinner at Marian Wright Edelman's house in Washington, DC. After a gracious welcome and delicious dinner, Ms. Edelman asked about the possibility of launching a motherhood movement in the US, a motherhood movement that would not leave out poor women. We recognized that night that it was essential for the success of a motherhood movement that we focus on our common ground.

We left that meeting determined to host dinners in our communities, to ask other mothers about their concerns, and, most of all, to take the voices of mothers seriously in our living rooms so that they will be taken seriously in our government. Within six months of that meeting, there was increased activity among mothers, and I realize that the motherhood movement began long before that meeting. I am especially delighted that so many new organizations proudly include "mother" in their names. Here are a few more.

For those who want to delve more deeply into the academics of mothering, you'll be pleased to know about the Centre for Research on Mothering at York University, Toronto, which houses the Association for Research on Mothering and the *Journal of the Association for Research on Mothering*. The center's mandate is "to promote feminist maternal scholarship by building and sustaining a community of researchers—academics and grassroots—interested in the topic of mothering-motherhood." Andrea O'Reilly is the director of the center, which provides yearly conferences, regular seminars, and ongoing publications as well as curriculum for teaching motherhood.

Encouraging research on mothers has helped to provide us with a greater understanding of the economic issues of mothering. In her book *The Price of Motherhood,* Ann Crittenden argues persuasively for an economic appreciation of the work of mothers. Crittenden's group, Mothers Ought to Have Equal Rights (MOTHERS), is "a grassroots mothers' movement to improve the economic status of mothers and others who care for family dependents." The website of the group is *www.mothersoughttohaveequalrights.org.*

Another group concerned with the economic status of mothers, among other things, is Mothers & More (*www.mothersandmore.org*). This group "cares for the caregiver." They provide a nationwide network of local chapters for "mothers who are—by choice or circumstance—altering their participation in the paid workforce over the course of their active parenting years." The group serves mothers at home as well as mothers working outside the home. Mothers & More "champions the value and necessity of all mothers' work to our society—paid and unpaid, within and outside of the home."

Another group interested in public policy and political action is Mothers Acting Up (*www.mothersactingup.org*). This group is dedicated to "mobilizing the gigantic political strength of Mothers." "We realize that we live in a world that does not prioritize or protect our children's well-being and that this will not change without each of us finding the courage and commitment to speak out on their behalf." I was invited to speak this year at a Mother's Day parade organized by Mothers Acting Up in Albuquerque. I was thrilled to find out about this political action group for mothers and delighted that its members had such a great sense of humor. The event I attended was a parade, not a march. The signs were held up with balloons. People wore funny hats. At the parade last year in Boulder, where the group originated, the founders wore costumes and walked on stilts.

Mothers Acting Up celebrates the original meaning of Mother's Day with parades in cities all over the US. The day was created by Julia Ward Howe in the mid-1800s as a day of peace. In her original proclamation, Howe said, "In the name

of womanhood and humanity, I earnestly ask that a general
congress of women without limit of nationality, may be
appointed and held at someplace deemed most convenient
and the earliest period consistent with its objects to promote the alliance of the different nationalities, the amicable
settlement of international questions, the great and general
interests of peace."

I hope that this general congress of women is building.
I pray that mothers are gathering in towns and cities all
over the US to talk of peace and the common good. Already
there's a website for the motherhood movement: *www.moth-
ersmovement.org.* The Mothers Movement Online (MMO)
provides "resources for mothers and others who think
about social change." It provides "an open source for the
distribution of information about social, cultural, economic
and political conditions that impact the lives of mothers."
It serves as a "clearinghouse for resources and ideas that
support social change to improve the status of mothers and
others who are responsible for care work in our society."

MMO, MOTHERS, and Mothers & More raise important
questions about mothering and caregiving. How can we balance work and family life without losing job status? How can
the job of rearing children be shared more equitably by men
and by more members of society? Do mothers at home have
to face economic hardship in old age because they don't have
enough Social Security?

Groups like the Motherhood Project, Mothers' Support
Network, and MOCHA are asking questions about the social
fabric of society. What kind of societal values, organizations,
and institutions help to support children, mothers, families?
What is the proper relationship of commercialism and materialism to children and family life? These increasing efforts
to proudly raise the flag of motherhood for social, economic,
and political efforts bode well for the voices of women. It is
the voice of the feminine that we need today.

In an ancient Hindu story, just as the world is about to be
destroyed, the gods remember a legend that says that when
the world is about to be defeated, it is only a woman who
can save it. They summon Durga, and she defeats powerful

enemies with the help of the ferocious goddess who leaps from her forehead at the last crucial minute. This legend demonstrates feminine power and reminds us that even at the last moment, we have resources we hardly imagined. These organizations are such resources. They are the stirrings of the renaissance. The murmuring of our collective voices has begun. Let yours be heard. As Maggie Kuhn said, "Speak your mind even if your voice shakes." These groups will help keep yours steady.

From Mothering, *issue no. 119 (July–August 2003).*

lee's bed

MY CHILDREN ARE ALL GROWN UP. My youngest just turned 21, and my oldest is nearly 30. Reaching the "twos" with your children is a lot like teaching them to swim. When my four were toddlers, I was eager for the day when they all knew how to swim because I worried about them when they were around water. With adult children, it's not the water that you worry about so much—it's the whole world. Toddlers are learning how to navigate in the world; adult children are that world. Parenting adults feels like starting over again, as you learn how to talk to your children as emotional equals. It helps if you've been doing so all along.

My adult children are still part of my world, and we all get together frequently. Three of them have lived at home on and off during their 20s. We have a big house, and the job market has been challenging. In addition to the economic justification, however, I simply like the fact that my children still live at home at times. It's been the kind of slow and gentle weaning for me as a mom that I gave to them as infants and toddlers. I was reassured when I heard that in Europe young adults are expected to take until their 30s to find themselves. I understand that in Latin America it is common for adult children to live at home until they are married. And, of course, I remember John Boy and *The Waltons*.

But still sometimes I worry, because we do things differently. I don't have nice, easy, linear stories about my children to tell other adults my age who brag to me about theirs. The directions my adult children's lives have taken, like their

educations, have been nonconformist. They are individuals. During the days that we homeschooled, the motto of our
school was "Every experience carries its lesson," from *Dune*.
Why am I now surprised when their education as adults mirrors the successful self-teaching of their younger years?

And why am I surprised that we should have such a
gradual weaning, if a weaning it is at all? Raising my children
in an atmosphere of cooperation rather than coercion has
preserved our bond of attachment into adulthood. We really
like one another. And how odd it is that we must ask ourselves
if it is OK to be so close.

In so many families, the 18th year is a rigidly enforced
rite of passage out of the home and into the world. It is often
enforced with no gradations, as a once-and-for-all kind
of thing. I know parents who move to a smaller house or
remodel their child's bedroom as soon as the child is 18, as
if he or she will never come back again. No wonder so many
don't. That has not been my experience, however. Like the
teens who crowded our house during those years, I have come
to believe that it is perfectly natural for our home to be a flex-
ible refuge during the early years of adulthood as well.

Still, we sit on my bed in the morning and sometimes talk
about how unusual it is that we all get along so well. Or is it?
On vacation recently, we were sitting on the porch of a rental
house and noticed that three of us were sitting in exactly the
same relation to one another as we do on my bed in the mornings. We have this habit of intimacy.

Later during the vacation, I went out to dinner with Lee,
Cyndee, Andei, and Ocean. We are women who have known
one another for 10 to 20 years and have raised our children
pretty much the same way, in a spirit of trust and cooperation.
We did our best to follow our children's lead and to trust the
natural way of less intervention and more interaction.

After dinner, my friends and I went to drop off Lee at her
house and ended up sitting on her bed talking. I wondered,
as the children gathered and joined the four of us women
on the bed, what was going on. Cyndee's and Lee's preteen
sons joined us on the bed, nuzzling and cuddling just like
little puppies, as Cyndee called them. They were acting like

animals, after all. One young boy caught my eye as if to ask if this was all OK with me, too, this nuzzling and rolling and frolicking about. It was. It was just like our house. Soon after the interlude on Lee's bed, I attended the La Leche League International (LLLI) conference in San Francisco, where Marian Tompson, a founder of LLLI, showed me a photo of her great-grandchild. She proudly showed me the young parents and commented that it had been a natural birth. Four generations of natural births, four generations of homebirths.

The conversations with my children on my bed, the sweet evening on Lee's bed, the pictures of Marian's great-grandchild help me remember that something very profound is happening. At the same time we are discouraged that social change in support of healthy families is taking so long, we are already there. We are weaving with an evolutionary thread that goes back in time to traditional societies.

Fifty years ago, La Leche League took up this thread, inspired by physicians such as Grantly Dick-Read and Gregory White, who trusted the natural way and knew that it was fear, not childbirth or breastfeeding, that was the problem. While it seems that we've been advocating childbirth reform and parents' rights forever, in fact most social movements take 100 years to become established. The civil rights movement, the movement for jails instead of lynching, and the movement for public schools all took about 100 years to accomplish their goals. After 50 years, natural birth and parenting are considered legitimate choices; now it is time for assimilation.

Why is this so important? Isn't it arrogant to talk of people assimilating the natural way? Isn't the natural way just another lifestyle choice? No, it's not. That's the point, really. While many people think of natural choices, particularly about birth and parenting, as just another lifestyle choice, they are, in fact, health choices. They are health choices because current scientific evidence supports the safety and superiority of the natural way.

Natural choices help protect the integrity of pregnancy and birth, the first environment. Arguments for natural pregnancy and birth are often framed in free-choice rhetoric and give women the impression that doing things naturally is some

kind of self-sacrifice. This couldn't be further from the truth. It
is because the natural way is, in fact, so self-generating that we
recommend it to one another in the first place.

During natural birth, for example, an intricate chemistry
of hormones provides pain relief, moves the baby through the
uterus, and prepares the mother to welcome the baby. This
intricate chemistry also unlocks in the birthing woman a dormant instinctual intelligence that informs her as a new mother.
Chemical agents, such as the drugs given to most women during childbirth in this country, disrupt this intricate chemistry
of natural birth and instead set the birthing woman's body into
a fight-or-flight response. Thus, most women in the US give
birth under stress when it doesn't have to be that way.

While women believe they are making free choices about
birth, no one tells them that taking drugs during labor might
adversely affect their bonding with and affection for their
babies. No one tells them that the drugs might put their babies
at risk for later drug addiction. No one tells them that there
are nondrug alternatives for pain relief or that the simple
presence of another woman during birth will dramatically
reduce their desire for pain medication. We talk about free
choice, but little choice is actually available in the monopoly
that is technological and pharmaceutical hospital birth. While
scientific evidence shows that birth is safe in any setting, only
1 percent of births in the US take place outside of a hospital.
What birthing women in the US consider free choice is actually a constructed reality offering little actual choice.

This same monopoly turns women's pregnancies into medical events, with routine prenatal tests that were once reserved
for special circumstances and that parents acquiesce to all too
casually. No one tells mothers that these tests are not recommended for routine use and that scientific evidence does not
support their routine use. No one tells them that the jury is
still out on ultrasound. We know now that ultrasound changes
the cells of the baby, but we don't know what this means.
Because of the high-risk treatment afforded normal pregnancies, a woman prepares for her child in nervous anticipation
rather than the ecstatic joy that is her birthright, and that
is just what her baby needs to grow best. Studies show that

mothers who are stressed during early pregnancy give birth to more aggressive children.

If I appear to screech about the natural way, it's not because I want to form a cult or a club or to feel good because we're all doing things the same way. It's simply because I know that women are being sold a bill of goods, a limited sense of their own capacities, a distorted view of birth. And the tragedy is that their choices are not just simple lifestyle choices but choices that will affect the health of their babies and themselves for decades to come. Women should be encouraged to trust in the innate integrity of the process of birth and in its transformative nature. By surrendering to it, they come out renewed. As the birth and the moments following it set the tone for the interaction with the baby and therefore the future health of the baby, women deserve and need to be undisturbed during pregnancy and birth so that the dyad of mother and baby will operate optimally.

I realized on Lee's bed that this way of natural, undisturbed birth is the precursor for our entire parenting adventure. Birth is perhaps the first moment that we try out the trust we will need to mother our babies. We trust that a baby knows how to be born, that our bodies know what to do. We cooperate with our bodies and our babies. We take our babies into our arms and carry them around with us everywhere. We sleep with them and nurse them until they stop. And when they have temper tantrums, lie, and climb out of windows, we trust that they are basically good. Trust and love create a stronger bond than fear and control. We learn early on that children, like everyone else, have good reasons for their behavior and that simply spending more time with them usually cures most ills. And we practice putting family first and putting people before things. We trust our inner authority, and we recognize that our children have one as well.

Years ago, when I read *Liberated Parents, Liberated Children* by Adele Faber and Elaine Mazlish, I was terrified because the way I wanted to parent was going to require me to stop trying to control my children. I was not always going to be able to have my way. I was going to have to cooperate. It was hard to do this. It was like learning a new language, this language of trust and cooperation. But slowly, this process begin to have its own rewards, and I became more satisfied with the cooperation of intimate family life than I had been with the solitary role of authoritarian leader.

Many others have discovered these same truths, threads that wend their way back to traditional societies and to truths about human nature that are not new but only rediscovered and renamed for modern times. We now have second, third, and fourth generations of parents in the US who have learned to trust themselves and their children and the natural process of life. There are enough of us now to report back that the kids turn out just fine. And that the added and perhaps unanticipated joy is that the bonding and attachment of the early years provide a rich foundation for a lifetime of love. It's hard to imagine, when your child is an infant, that your loving respect is creating the grounds for a real friendship with your adult child, but it is. It really is.

From Mothering, *issue no. 120 (September–October 2003).*

wake up!

I WANT TO RUN TO THE ROOFTOPS to yell a warning to US women: Watch out! Wake up! You're in danger. This summer the Centers for Disease Control and Prevention (CDC) released the most recent cesarean rates, and the 2002 average of 26.1 percent is the highest rate in US history. At least four times as many women die of causes related to cesarean birth as those related to vaginal birth. What this cesarean rate really means is that the number of women dying in childbirth is on the rise. As always, poor and minority women are overrepresented in these numbers. Tragically, a woman's chance of dying during pregnancy or birth in the US has not decreased significantly in more than 25 years.

The revealing thing about these statistics is that where a woman lives may be her greatest risk factor for a cesarean. Of the 18 areas with the highest cesarean rates, 11 are in the South and 7 are in the East. Puerto Rico has the highest rate, 44.7 percent, and the next three highest are Mississippi at 31.1 percent, New Jersey at 30.9 percent, and Louisiana at 30.4 percent. Of the 18 states with the lowest rates, 10 are in the West and 5 in the Midwest: Utah at 19.1 percent, New Mexico at 19.1 percent, Alaska at 19.4 percent, and Idaho at 19.7 percent.

These statistics are very disillusioning. Many of us have worked for childbirth reform for more than 30 years, only to feel that we are losing ground. Have we not done a good enough job of educating mothers? Have mothers themselves come to accept technological, surgical birth as normal? Is the practice of defensive medicine so widespread that evidence-based care is just impossible?

In many ways, we have failed new mothers with the illusion of free choice. In my generation, fathers were not allowed in the delivery room, women's hands and feet were routinely strapped down, and silver nitrate was applied to the baby's eyes immediately after birth. In my generation, we had no choices. The concept of informed consent was not widely known, and the rights of hospital patients were unheard of. It was generally assumed that if you gave birth in a hospital, you would have to comply with questionable practices. This was in the seventies, when feminism informed a generation of women about hidden societal oppression and empowered us to believe in ourselves.

Now we believe that we're already liberated. Young, vulnerable, pregnant women assume they are receiving evidence-based care. The reassurance that they can choose pain relief during labor if they want it or that they can even have a cesarean birth if they want one gives women the illusion of choice. In truth, the choices are meaningful only within a very limited context of interventionist and therefore unsafe birth. In light of normal birth, they are pitiful gestures from a system in which the illusion of choice is the only real standard.

Where is our insistence on real standards for normal birth, goals based on evidence, talk of the baby? In my generation, we talked of all decisions during pregnancy and birth in light of what effect they might have on the baby. It was assumed one would err on the side of caution. Now we don't always talk about the baby in relationship to drugs in labor, for example, or prenatal tests. Do we ask, "What effect might this ultrasound have on my baby?" Do we ask, "Will these anesthetic drugs I'm going to take during labor have an effect on my baby?" I read an article in the *New York Times* a couple of years ago espousing the virtues of "walking" epidurals. In the entire article, the word *baby* was not mentioned once. We act as if we believe that pregnancy and birth are the experiences of the mother alone and her body is simply a vehicle. What about the baby?

I think we have failed as childbirth educators because we've framed natural childbirth as just another choice rather than as the best choice. Natural childbirth is the best choice because it is the safest choice. It is safest because, by definition, it involves fewer medical interventions, and it is these interventions that contribute to at least 50 percent of maternal deaths.

We have also failed to produce enough midwives. While midwife-attended births have increased dramatically, from 1 percent in the 1970s to 10 percent today, there are simply not enough midwives. Despite the fact that all countries with better infant-mortality rates than the US use midwives as primary birth attendants, most women in the US associate them with inferior care. Even though studies consistently show that midwives use fewer interventions and have better birth outcomes than doctors, most women in the US can't easily find one.

It's very tempting to blame doctors for the high cesarean rate. Certainly, the distribution of cesarean rates suggests that local and regional standards of care affect the likelihood of interventions. Yet these variations in care are directly related to increasing medical and legal pressures on doctors. In 1970 the cesarean rate was 5 percent. By 1995 the rate had increased to 20.8 percent because of the changing definition of acceptable risk. Breech babies were routinely delivered vaginally before 1970, for example, and are now routinely delivered by cesarean. Many babies who might previously have been delivered using forceps are now candidates for cesarean birth. The increased use of the electronic fetal monitor, with its wide variations in interpretations, has caused more cesareans to be performed. In addition, abnormal labor has been diagnosed more frequently in the last 30 years. All of these reasons for the increased cesarean rate have to do with changes in doctors' practice, not changes in women's capacities.

The cesarean rate reached its previous high of 24.7 percent in 1988. At that time, efforts were made to reduce the number of repeat cesareans, which account for one-third of all cesareans, and vaginal births after cesareans (VBAC) were encouraged. The current high cesarean rate is expected to increase even more because many birth services and institutions are no longer making VBAC available due to increased legal and peer pressures. These pressures impede implementation of evidence-based practices recommended by the World Health

Organization (WHO) and the Coalition to Improve Maternity Services (CIMS), both of which recommend a VBAC rate of 75 percent. These organizations recommend a cesarean rate of between 10 and 15 percent, as does the federal government, which has set the goal of a 15 percent cesarean rate in the US.

Reluctantly, I blame the mothers. I blame women when we don't expect more of ourselves. I blame women when we believe we have a limited capacity. I blame women for being immobilized by cultural myths about birth. I blame women for acquiescing to a system that requires dependence and compliance. I blame women for not being willing to differentiate between prejudice and evidence. Think about it. Nature would not make a pregnant woman dependent. Nature would make her powerfully intuitive in response to the deepest needs of her baby, and it would equip the human female with everything she needs to birth normally. Nature would not make the biological process essential to the survival of our species fraught with danger. Nature would make it simple. And while birth is more successful in community, the human female is a self-contained biological imperative, able to give birth and feed her infant all by herself.

Woefully, American women don't believe this. When I tell women that the evidence shows that birth is safe in any setting—that is, birth is equally safe at home, in a birth center, or at the hospital—they nod hopefully, but I know they don't believe me. Admittedly, it's hard to believe that birth is normal when your community does not share this belief. It's human nature to be influenced by the beliefs of those around you, even if they are incorrect. When it comes to birth, most of us operate more on prejudice than on evidence. We simply do not believe that birth is normal because we have not been exposed to or have not experienced normal birth.

Instead, we believe erroneously that we have a right to pain-free birth. We are so accustomed to taking drugs for our pain that we do not recognize that pain is an ally during birth. While we would certainly expect and even require pain medication for physical injury, the pain of labor is bearable, short-lived, and part of the feedback system. Pain medication during labor puts the baby at unnecessary risk, and there is no medical evidence to support its use in normal birth. Perhaps most important, we can handle the pain. We are human females. We are *designed* to handle it.

When we cease to believe this, we are in trouble. Will we find our way back to normal birth in the US? Or will we go the way of South America, where cesarean rates are in the 50 to 80 percent range? We need older women to come forward to tell younger women their stories about normal birth. We need childbirth educators who are independent enough to tell families the truth about the politics of birth. And we need more midwives, the purveyors of normal birth. It's time that birthing women knew about the national and international health initiatives to determine evidence-based guidelines for maternal and newborn care. Both WHO and CIMS provide evidence-based percentages for the frequency of common obstetrical interventions. (See my book, *Having a Baby, Naturally*, Appendix 1: "Birth Report Card," page 291.)

Ask your practitioner what his or her individual cesarean rate is. Ask what the rate is for the practice. Ask about other interventions and how they compare to evidence or federal guidelines. If the question is balked at or not taken seriously, be cautious. Don't become a statistic. Individuals or practices proud of their statistics will be familiar with them and tell them to you in an instant.

We can't wait for doctors to change. Their medical, legal, and peer pressures do not allow them to practice evidence-based care. Our current standard of maternity care is based on considerations of patient preference, potential liability, and monetary concerns. It is not evidence-based and does not aspire to be. It aspires to be profitable. Revenues from health care are a cornerstone of our gross domestic product.

What we really need is an awakening of mothers. We need mothers who think more highly of themselves than to be subjected to experimental care. We need women who believe in the normalcy of birth. We need families to advocate for normal birth and for midwifery. In the 1980s it was citizen activism that advocated for vaginal birth after cesareans and ultimately lowered the cesarean rate. At that time there were many organizations and institutions advocating for normal birth and for homebirth: The National Association of Parents and Professionals for Safe Alternatives in Childbirth (NAPPSAC), Home Oriented Maternity Experience (HOME), Informed Homebirth (IH), Alternative Birth Coalition (ABC), and the Association for Childbirth at Home International (ACHI).

As always, it will be up to the women. I believe in women. Each woman contains the genetic blueprint for normal birth and can trust the inherent integrity of her biology. She has authoritative knowledge within her. Normal birth unlocks the mother's instinctual intelligence. We can use that intelligence to differentiate between prejudice and evidence. We can be mature enough to consider the needs of our babies during birth.

When we have a new baby, his or her need to touch us and feed from us inconveniences us many times during the early months and years. During that time we are prepared as new mothers to subjugate our needs because we realize that our babies are more vulnerable than we are. During birth it's the same. Just as we did during pregnancy, we continue to make choices during birth that assure the safest and healthiest environment for the baby. That means enduring labor full on, no holding back, and protecting the baby with our courage from the potential harm of questionable interventions. As the baby grows, there will be many times we will be unable to protect him or her from harm. Birth is one time that we can. It's what this rite of passage is all about.

From Mothering, *issue no. 121 (November–December 2003).*

slow lane

IN THE MORNINGS I LOVE TO WATCH the birds frolic on the feeders outside my bedroom window. I put seed, suet, and water out for them. In late fall, there are red-shafted flickers, hairy woodpeckers, finches, chickadees, nuthatches, and of course jays. Sometimes there are hawks in the air, and always ravens at the compost. This summer we had our usual share of raccoons, who also love the bird food and groom themselves in the water. We saw so many squirrels at the feeders this summer that we took to naming them. Deer and bear furtively enjoy our flowers and fruit trees.

I learn a lot from these animals and from their habits during the changing seasons here. There's a resilience, a steadiness, a survival that inspires. The animals and the woods are my companions and recognize me as I pass by. I love living in the country and have done so most of my adult life. Recently I read of a New Mexico artist who describes herself as a homebody and leads, "a simple, solitary life." I admire that.

I also loved being at home with my children. I value the life of the home: a long conversation by the fire, a walk in the neighborhood, sitting at the table after a satisfying meal, relaxing baths and bedtime routines, home-cooked food and honest relationships. I recently had the opportunity to be at home for a time and saw anew how rich the life of the home really is, how much we miss when we hurry through it to other things.

Life at home can easily take our full-time attention. Adding work, family, friends, and other social obligations, as well as ever-developing new interests, leaves us all feeling that we can never catch up. We believe we can do all the things we think of, and we never stop thinking of something new. From the vantage point of someone who likes driving in the slow lane these days, could it be that we are suffering from yet another addiction of our fast-paced society? Could it be that we're addicted to being busy? It feels like an addiction, doesn't it? There's that unsettled feeling when we're not busy—the social pressure to be busy, the painful transition to a slower life.

I remember that as a young mom with three children under five, I was going so fast that I couldn't slow down. Even when I had an opportunity to relax, I kept doing things. I was in overdrive. There's a rhythm and chemistry of overdrive that's seductive and exciting, that keeps us from feeling other things. And with little ones, it can be a necessity. Here's a parody I wrote 15 years ago when I was a young mom to help me put my own busy life in perspective:

busy and efficiency

Busy and Efficiency have been in town again. You know, it's always fun to see those two at first. They give me a rush of excitement. But, boy, they sure do wear me out. I spend all of my time showing them around town, but they're always ready to see more. During their latest visit, we went to all the museums, took in many pueblo dances, saw all of the movies and shows in town, and ate at most of the restaurants. And it's not even tourist season.

These two don't seem to care about sleep. I think the only time they slow down is when they're sick, and then only long enough to take something. Busy, for example, would rather use sleep to make plans for the next day, and she never has time to remember her dreams. She's planning before her eyes are even open.

Busy is beautiful, light, and bouncy, with long blond hair that flows around in a circle when she turns her head—which she does often, as she is always looking around. Efficiency looks like a cross between my seventh-grade grammar teacher, the spinster Miss Ellis, and Ichabod Crane. Her nose is long and pointed, she wears

sensible suits, and she always carries a pencil perched
behind her ear.

I would like it if Busy and Efficiency just had the social
graces to know when they had overstayed their welcome.
When they're here, they often interfere with my relation-
ships with my other friends. For example, my friend Poetry
has been wanting to get together so we can go over some
of our latest work. But when Efficiency and Busy are in
town, they expect me to give them my full attention, and
of course I do. I haven't yet learned how to say no to them.
They intoxicate me with their ideas. It always seems, at
least at the time, that the latest idea they've come up with
is more entrancing than the last, and that if I get involved
with just this one more thing, the world will be saved.
Meanwhile, my personal life is falling apart, and the other
things I value are taking a backseat.

Well, I can't go on like this for long, now that I've recog-
nized their subtle seduction. The question is how to stand
up to them. I know when my boyfriend gets back from his
trip, I will be able to put Busy and Efficiency on hold for
a while, but this time I want to do it myself. This time I
want to meet some new friends who can teach me how to
balance the time I spend with Busy and Efficiency. I hear
there are some new kids in town named Play, Relaxation,
and Leisure. I'll ask someone who knows them to introduce
us. I'll bet that my children know them.

There's a commonality to our conspiracy to be busy. We
all expect one another to be busy and are suspicious of people
who aren't part of the technological culture, who don't have
an answering machine or who refuse to get e-mail. Like seeing
the emperor's new clothes, as long as we are *all* too busy, it's
acceptable.

We don't even let ourselves off the hook when we're sick.
People routinely come to work sick, and if they do take time
off, they take off just a day or so. Over-the-counter drugs
and television ads suggest that we should just take something to get back to normal quick. Is illness only a nuisance

with no value, our only task to banish all signs of it quickly
and to forge on even when we're weak? We treat ourselves
like machines.

So much has changed since I was a young mother. At that
time we lived in an area where phone service was scarce, and
we were part of an eight-party line. In the early days of the
magazine, I wrote my editorials on an electric typewriter, and
our only other machine was a copier. Years later we added a
fax machine and, gradually, computers, e-mail, and of course
voice mail. With so many communication devices, we are
expected to be plugged in. Yes, perhaps we're more efficient,
and we're certainly more busy, but we're also more pressured.
In the days of the eight-party line, we didn't expect instant
replies. Now we do.

That pressure to "be all that you can be" keeps us from
simply being. While new magazines extol the virtues of
the simple life, that generally only means buying different
products, not changing one's lifestyle or consciousness. Living simply means doing both. Living in the slow lane means
having the courage to measure the success of the day by a
good meal or an intimate conversation. It means structuring
your own day, leading with your own impulses. Living simply
means coming home.

I have borrowed my idea of living in the slow lane from the
international Slow Food movement, a movement started in
Italy to protest McDonald's in the historic plazas. It has cap-
tured people's desire for a simpler life and has spread around
the world. Since I've been living in the slow lane, I've noticed a
change in my physiology. I am more in tune with my sensitivities. Things I handled routinely in the past actually upset me
more than I realized. I notice that I often try to do too much
in a day, then measure my success by whether or not I got
"everything done." I can set an impossible standard for myself
and, to keep up, must always remain on alert. Like most of us,
I pedal faster but still don't get there. A friend whom I rarely
see called recently and said, in response to the possibility of
getting together, "I can't be extremely social. There's just too
much to do. Treadmilling, you know." I do know.

I wonder if we really want to live like this, and if not,

how to find our way back. How can we unplug, not just
from TV but also from a cultural ethic of constant stimulation and action?

This summer a researcher in neonatology told me that
aggressive behavior in children could be traced to prenatal
stress. The dramatic increase in premature births may also be
related to stress. Are we passing on our stress to our babies?
What does the pace of our society do to our physiology and to
that of our children?

During my recent cocoon stage, I have been somewhat free
from commercial messages and outside solicitations. Phone,
mail, and e-mail are now mostly solicitations. Less input
creates a certain peacefulness and allows for contemplation.
What place does contemplation have in our world? Do we
ever ask our children if they had time to contemplate today?
How do we make sense of our own lives and improve our own
behavior if we do not have an opportunity for contemplation
and reflection?

The point of reflecting on the pace of society is not to push
back the clock but to ask a very simple question. Who are we?
Are we imperfect beings who must be controlled, manipulated, and improved through elective cesareans, cosmetic surgery, cloning, pharmaceutical drugs, and a host of things that
others think we should have? Or are we instead perfect beings
who can trust in the moment and the integrity of life as it is? I
find it much more challenging to accept life as it is.

I look hard for the rightness in things as they are. I want
to make room for the simple things. And not just different
products, but a different way of doing things—taking time
to do things, doing fewer things but doing them well, leaving
time for the unexpected, and not having to rush. Doing things
this way is not a throwback to the past, it is a discipline. It is
a discipline of deciding what comes first in our lives. When
technology allows everyone, from friends to solicitors, to have
equal access to our lives, then it is only we who can sort out
who and what comes first. And in weighing and measuring,
we must not forget the often unspoken but essential life of
the home, a life that, without our attention, deteriorates and
contributes to social chaos.

It's hard to change lanes, to put personal life first, knowing that others still plugged in will expect unrealistic things from us. Yet it is the unchecked activity in our lives and in our society that encourages excess. A principle of balance embodies giving to others as we give to ourselves. In a balanced life, there is contraction as well as expansion.

It's as if we're making room for negative space, for things to happen. When we're all full up and scheduled, the mystery doesn't happen the way it does so easily when we're traveling, for example, and taking things as they come.

The simple life has the possibility of adventure, of changing our minds, of surprise. In the slow lane, we will not miss the magic.

From Mothering, *issue no. 122 (January–February 2004).*

instead of hitting

AT A MEETING I ATTENDED RECENTLY, I mentioned an
article we wanted to solicit entitled "Instead of Hitting." One
woman asked what the title meant. Another said, "But doesn't
the Bible tell us to hit our kids?" Later in the conversation,
when I questioned the wisdom of time-outs, people were even
more confused. Well, if we don't hit or *punish*—I could hear
them all wonder silently—then what *are* we supposed to do?
These are legitimate concerns. When I was a new mom 30
years ago, I had these same questions.

I started out hitting my kids. I would lose my temper when
their behavior got out of my control, and I would hit. I never
felt good about it, but I didn't know what else to do, and I
thought it was effective because afterward I had regained control of the situation. I thought that I had to hit them because I
had to control them. Certainly, others expected that I should,
and I thought that was what parenting was all about. But it
just didn't feel right.

About the time that my third child was born, I saw a bumper sticker that read "People Are Not for Hitting and Children
Are People Too." I was flabbergasted because I believed this,
but I was still hitting my children. I was waiting to discover
something else to do first and then to stop hitting. When I
saw the bumper sticker, I realized that I would just have to
stop. *Then* I would figure out what else to do. And I did.

I was initially inspired by a concept I heard at La Leche
League meetings: that discipline is based on loving guidance. Later I read the books *Liberated Parents, Liberated*

Children and *How to Talk So Kids Will Listen & Listen So Kids Will Talk,* by Adele Faber and Elaine Mazlish, and I had the opportunity to interview the authors. But their concepts were foreign to me. I embraced them intellectually but didn't have an emotional clue about how to implement them. I grew up in an authoritarian household, and my own upbringing was what I knew habitually.

The books of Faber and Mazlish are based on the work of the psychologist Haim Ginott, author of *Between Parent and Child.* What they all recommend is a fundamental paradigm shift from authoritarian parenting to cooperative parenting. In fact, in Dolores Curran's book *Traits of a Healthy Family,* she found that in healthy families, no one family member is dominant. While corporal punishment of children produces short-term obedience, it has long-term negative consequences on character and behavior. Research at the University of New Hampshire found that children who are rarely or never spanked have higher scores on cognitive tests than children who are frequently spanked.

But how do we change our habits and our beliefs? When I read *Liberated Parents, Liberated Children,* I was terrified. I felt totally out of control. It took me a while to realize that the control I achieved by spanking was an illusion. My children would learn to hide their bad behavior from me if I spanked them, but I could never ultimately control them, and they would learn to resent me. The only hope I had of truly "controlling" things—that is, of having my own needs met—was rooted in our relationship. It is ultimately the relationship of love and mutual respect that ensures socialized behavior.

We want to make sure that as parents we do teach our children to be effective socially. Others expect this of us as well. Our desire to control our children is often thus precipitated by our image of ourselves as good, caring parents. At times, our concern for our own image can affect our actions toward our children more than our concern for their welfare. Often when we spank, we do so because we just can't tolerate *our* children acting in such a way. Our pride is hurt.

I think loss of pride is little compared to the loss of intimacy with our children that comes when we spank and punish them. We have to be very honest with ourselves to shift to a paradigm of cooperation. We have to be willing to take responsibility in conflicts with our children and to acknowledge that our own attitudes or beliefs might be contributing to the problem. We can try not to take conflict personally but to see it as an opportunity to learn new information that will help us prevent future conflict. We must learn humility.

Being humble, however, does not mean that we give up our authority. A parent's authority is based not on being right all the time but on being the one in charge. You do not have to give up your authority as a parent or be permissive to parent in a more cooperative way. However, you do have to learn a new language, and it takes time. The more you practice cooperation, the more skilled at it you become.

What is this new language? What are the elements that help us discipline nonviolently with loving guidance and without punishment, time-outs, or spanking? They are words. They are attitudes. They are beliefs. They are demeanor. For example, the number-one trait of a healthy family is the ability to communicate and listen. Loving guidance implies that children, like adults, have good reasons for their behavior and that their cooperation can be engaged to solve problems.

How do we engage the cooperation of children? We talk to them in a different way.

Here are some examples of new ways to approach problems with our children:

- We can describe what we see.
  I see a glass near the edge of the table.
- We can describe the problem.
  The kitchen is a mess.
- We can give information.
  Bikes left out in the rain will rust.
- We can make a statement of appropriate function or behavior.
  We don't hit people.
- We can offer a choice.
  You can wear the red outfit or the green outfit.

- *We can say it in a word.*
  Shoes!
- We can describe what we feel.
  When I come home tired from work, I feel sorry for myself when I have to make dinner. It would be so nice to come home to dinner being cooked and to have some help in the kitchen.
- We can write a note.

The communication suggestions above stand in sharp contrast to poor communication, which blames, accuses, calls names, threatens, commands, lectures, warns, evokes martyrdom, compares, is sarcastic, or prophesies. Notice the example under "We can describe what we feel," above. It encourages family members to come forward to help. It is an "I" message and talks totally about the speaker's feelings without accusing anyone else of anything. The word *you* is not in the sentence.

If instead a parent said something blaming and self-pitying, such as "I can't believe I have to come home so tired and make dinner, too. Why don't you ever make dinner for me? Why don't you ever help me? I have to do everything myself," family members would begrudgingly offer help, but they would be more likely to mentally focus on defending themselves than on the needy parent.

Communication is a skill we can always improve upon, and communicating means we have to get comfortable with strong emotions and be willing to talk about anything. Good communication is fostered by spending time talking together and by being sensitive to timing and context. And, perhaps most important, good communication requires that we learn to rebound from anger and to reconcile with others afterward.

To rebound from anger, we have to free ourselves of blame and judgment, even toward ourselves. It is easier to be tolerant of others when we are tolerant of ourselves. In fact, it helps to have a kind of radical self-acceptance and to trust in things as they are. This doesn't mean that we don't try to change things or to get our own needs met, but we do so with the compassionate understanding that we all have good, even if sometimes mistaken, reasons for our behavior.

When we appreciate that others have good reasons for their behavior, it allows us to approach them with love in our hearts. **That way we are more likely to frame our arguments in some of the ways that Haim Ginott suggested decades ago:**

- Express nuances of anger without nuances of insult.
- Talk to the situation, not the character of the person.
- Disagree without being disagreeable.
- Change a mood, not a mind.

When I was a new parent trying to figure out this new language of engaging cooperation, I put lists of suggestions like those above on my refrigerator. I put up a list of alternatives to punishment. The list helped me to remember new solutions instead of habitually relying on old, adversarial ones. Eventually I made these solutions my own. You will, too.

Here are some alternatives to punishment:

- Point out a way to be helpful.
- Express strong disapproval without attacking character.
- State your expectations.
- Show your child how to make amends.
- Take action.
- Allow your child to experience the consequences of his or her own behavior.
- Sympathize with the child. Be compassionate but stick to your decision.
- Give an early warning.
- Be specific. Tell what to clean up, not just to "clean up."
- Ask your child if you can help.
- Ignore some annoying behavior. Don't reinforce negative behavior by giving it too much attention.
- Do nothing.
- Tackle one problem, one behavior at a time.
- Use your sense of humor.
- Give yourself time to grow and change.

- Be affectionate.
- Make sure the children are getting enough sleep.
- Use the Golden Rule for children. Do unto them as you would like to have done unto you.
- Convey respect.
- Overlook differences that don't really matter.
- Don't do for your children what they can do for themselves.
- Schedule family time.
- Use "I" statements.
- Don't reward inappropriate behavior.
- Use encouragement and honest praise rather than blanket praise.
- Stop and think before you act.
- Don't make a big fuss over spills and accidents.
- Acknowledge positive behavior.
- Sometimes just listen and be sympathetic—to both sides.
- Be willing to change your mind.
- Say "yes" as much as possible.
- Get support and inspiration as a parent.
- Continue to think of your child as an emotional equal, and figure it out.
- Just say "no" to spanking.

At the end of the day, we want to preserve healthy, intimate relationships with our children into adulthood while also giving them correct guidance during childhood. As the parent of adult children, my experience has been that a good way to do this is by engaging cooperation rather than by hitting or punishing. Some would argue that this method dilutes authority, but that hasn't been my experience. It has been my ability to take responsibility as a parent, not harsh discipline, that has given me authority with my children. Harsh discipline produces compliance based on fear, which is not as binding as voluntary cooperation based on affection.

When I get confused about discipline, I think about what

I would do in a similar situation with an adult friend. I would
not slap my adult friend, for example, for spilling her drink. I
would assume that she made an honest mistake. I would not
punish my friend for acting immaturely in a group. Instead, I
would try to understand and sympathize, would give her the
benefit of the doubt, and would be eager to hear her side of
the story. We give our friends a wide berth because we do not
feel responsible for their behavior in the same way we do for
our children's behavior. It requires a huge leap of faith to trust
our children to their own destinies while we also guide them
through ours. We love our children more than anyone else on
earth, and we want to give them tools to be effective in the
world. It makes sense to model compassion. It works.

From Mothering, *issue no. 127 (November–December 2004).*

a lantern for lorri

IN ISSUE 119, I WROTE AN EDITORIAL, "Gathering the Mothers," about what I sense is a burgeoning mothers' movement in the US. In the editorial, I mentioned many of the organizations advocating for the concerns of mothers, including the National Association of Mothers' Centers (NAMC). As a result of this editorial, I was invited to participate in a panel at the 2004 NAMC conference last November. The panel, "Voices of Today's Mothers' Movement," also included Enola Aird, founder and director of the Motherhood Project; Ann Crittenden, author of *The Price of Motherhood* and a founder of the Mothers Ought to Have Equal Rights (MOTHERS) initiative; and Judith Stadtman Tucker, founder and editor of the Mothers Movement Online. While we each offered a different perspective on the idea of a mothers' movement, we were all in agreement that one was needed.

What does it mean to say that there is a mothers' movement afoot? Does it mean that women will develop a new consciousness about themselves as mothers? Does it mean that the voices of mothers will be heard more often in the national conversation? Does it mean that mothers will work together to advocate for social change? Yes, a mothers' movement can mean all of the above.

Will a mothers' movement be something centralized, based on the collective action of many individuals and groups working for one goal? Does it already exist in a nascent form, as something decentralized that informs the work of the many mothers' organizations working independent of but

complementary to each other? True to a feminine model, I
suspect a mothers' movement will be amorphous, hatching
and flying off in many directions but aimed at one thing: that
the voices of mothers be heard.

A mothers' movement is a movement toward social justice
for mothers, children, and families. What historical perspective can guide us in a mothers' movement? Is such a movement possible? Author and environmentalist Paul Hawken
puts us in good company. He reports that nearly 200,000
groups—more groups than at any other time in history—are
working worldwide for social justice. He predicts that "we the
people" are the next superpower.

We can also look for guidance at the history of feminism,
particularly at what has been called maternal feminism. The
efforts of early feminists focused not only on the right to vote
but also on larger issues of social justice, such as violence in
the home and alcoholism. A mothers' movement also draws
on the traditions of faith communities that work for social
justice; the Catholic Worker Movement, founded in 1933 by
Dorothy Day and Peter Maurin, is an example. And our movement is inspired, as are all social justice movements, by the
civil rights movement and Martin Luther King Jr.

What does the idea of a mothers' movement mean to
our personal lives? While we may not think of our everyday
struggles as mothers as part of a larger movement for social
justice, they are. Even so, those of us with young children can
rightly feel overwhelmed by the prospect of any responsibilities beyond these everyday struggles. For those of us with
older children, however, the timing could be just right for
more involvement in the political scene. A mothers' movement implies that more action will be required, but what really
will be needed is more consciousness.

When I think of a mothers' movement, I don't think of only
one organizing group or one cause. I think of a vast array of
networks, a web of organizations working to increase awareness and to influence social change. All parts of the web are
important, just as all kinds of social action are important. A
mothers' movement is really about finding and expressing

your voice as a mother. Here are some actions you can take to feel part of a mothers' movement. Some take only a little time, but their results are long-lasting. Others are easier to accomplish when children are older. All are valuable. You can perform them in sequence or just pick and choose.

See your mothering as a political act. The way you talk to your child becomes his or her inner voice. The way you model acceptance of your own body becomes the way your daughter learns to accept hers. The way you model the distribution of chores in the household provides a blueprint for your children's marriages. Bringing consciousness and awareness to the small acts of your life with your family can change the world. Your mothering is enough.

If you feel you have time for more and want support for yourself as a mother, have conversations with other mothers. Talk on the phone. Get together informally. Don't underestimate the importance of getting perspective on your own life by sharing common concerns with other mothers.

You may want to formalize your conversations with other mothers by joining or starting a group for mothers in your area. When I was a young mom, I found a family of support in my La Leche League (LLL) group. Today, in addition to LLL, mothers can join groups through the NAMC, Holistic Moms Network, Mothers' Support Network, Parents Support Network, Families for Natural Living, and Attachment Parenting International.

Some mothers' groups have started physical centers in their towns. Natural Resources in San Francisco and Mothers' Support Network in Sacramento are two examples of mothers' centers that offer retail products, both to bring in funds and to provide more services to parents. Turning your group into a mothers' center with a physical location can be challenging, but the process may be attractive to moms with an entrepreneurial spirit or business expertise.

Write letters to the editor. This may sound simple, but it is a great way to bring important issues to the attention of your community. The practice of writing letters improves your ability to make an argument and to articulate your thoughts

on important issues. It is also something you can do with a
baby. I started as a writer by writing letters to the editor of
our local paper in Alamogordo, New Mexico, when I was a
new mom.

**Get involved in advocacy groups that support your
favorite causes.** Go to the meetings of political parties in
your area. Find out how things happen, how bills are passed,
what groups have influence. Bring your school-age children to
visit your state legislature.

Educate yourself about the political process. Visit your
state and US representatives at their offices in your town and
develop a relationship with one of their staffers. Think about
an issue of importance to you, an issue that impacts your
family and families like yours. Educate yourself about the issue
and ask for your representative's help in working on it.

Run for office. You may not want to think about this until
your kids are older, at which point it may be the perfect thing
to do. With all your experience as a manager at home, you
are quite qualified for the multitasking involved with legisla-
tive work.

Strike a balance between shoring up your own family life
and contributing to society as a whole. If a mothers' movement is about hearing the voices of mothers, those voices will
be varied and distinct. In fact, I think the surprise of a mothers' movement could be that it wouldn't look like one thing.
It would not be easy to pin down and easily dismiss. It would
have many leaders.

As mothers, we think that our concerns are the concerns
of the many. We have to make sure that they are. As mothers,
we hope that our children are protected by society. We have
to act when they are not. As mothers, we have authoritative
knowledge about our own experience, an experience we have
in common with millions of women. We can build a more just
society on the ground of this common experience.

Our common experience as mothers, however, does not
guarantee that we will agree on everything. That doesn't matter. We may have differences of opinion about abortion, for
example, but may agree that all children should have access
to health care. We may disagree about gun ownership, for

example, but agree that special interests should not dominate politics. And while we may be of different faiths and spiritual practices, we would certainly agree that all families in the US should have adequate shelter and enough to eat.

The values of a just society do not belong to any political party. They are the values of the people. It is my fervent hope that we women, as mothers, will have the courage and equanimity to give one another reciprocal liberty, mutual accommodation. A mothers' movement perhaps could be based not so much on our shared values as on indifference to our unshared values.

When we look at the challenges that any organized effort requires, it seems to me that overlooking our differences in favor of our common ground will help us circumvent the challenges we will face as a social movement. Can we give one another this kind of wide berth in a mothers' movement? Can we be cooperative rather than competitive? Can we overlook our differences?

What kind of dynamics and leadership do we need? We need the dynamics of migrating geese. These wise birds have a variety of leaders, and when one tires another takes the lead. We need the causes of many mothers, not of one. We are strong in our diversity.

Regarding diversity, how do we broaden participation in a mothers' movement? How does it move from elite intellectualism to arguments that mothers from all walks of life can relate to? What are the mechanisms by which we include more diverse populations of mothers in a mothers' movement?

And with so many diverse populations of mothers involved, how do we overcome fragmentation? Or do we? The beauty of our movement is that it is made up of many different groups with many different goals. How can we come together when necessary for common goals without losing our individual identities and particular concerns?

In what is loosely called the mothers' movement, there can be no progress in polarized positions. Social change will be produced not by moral revelation but by shared experiences. The secret to our success will be in forging unexpected alliances.

When I went to the NAMC meeting, I hoped to make

alliances with other individuals and organizations. As a magazine, *Mothering* can help foster the agendas of diverse groups by letting our readers and website viewers know about them. We put up weekly activism alerts for nonprofit advocacy groups. As an editor, I want to provide a clearinghouse of information for mothers. And as a mother, I pray we will all get along. Society needs our voice—voices of compassion, of empathy, of mediation—now.

At the conference, NAMC cofounder Lorri Slepian and I talked about wanting to peer into the future of the mothers' movement so that we could foster its development. I realize now that we do not have to see the way to take the steps. We can trust that we are serving a larger purpose, a purpose that may not be fulfilled in one generation. Nonetheless, it is a purpose worthy of our efforts. It is time now for women to save the world. We need to hear the voices of mothers. Mothers' common experiences of making ends meet, seeing all sides of the story, and cultivating optimism can help us all right now.

From Mothering, *issue no. 128 (January–February 2005).*

mothers and fathers

BEFORE 1970, FATHERS PACED HOSPITAL waiting rooms handing out cigars as their wives labored alone. After the birth, they could see their new babies only from behind glass. Emboldened by the natural-childbirth renaissance of the 1970s, fathers changed all that when they demanded to participate in birth. At first they only watched the delivery, but soon they began to coach their wives during labor as well. Some lucky fathers even caught their babies. The role of the new father was forever changed.

In the 1980s, when I taught parenting classes for Family Week at the Omega Institute, mothers would complain to me that they had to drag their husbands along; few dads attended at all. By the time I taught my last class there, in the late 1990s, it was mostly couples who attended—fathers were not at all reluctant.

Men have lacked good role models. My grandfather never changed a diaper, never carried a baby. But by the 1990s, I saw men proudly wearing their babies in slings, carrying diaper bags and using them with authority. Men have come a long way from the detached parenting of the *Father Knows Best* era to become the responsive fathers of today.

Today's father is more actively involved than his grandfather and perhaps even his father. He is proud to have a fairly egalitarian relationship with his wife in which they share decision making, financial responsibilities, and household chores. While this "equality" is never cut-and-dried, most couples aspire to it.

Most couples also aspire to the equal sharing of parenting tasks. Some mothers even go so far as to bottle-feed so that their husbands, too, can feed the baby. Others work out complicated nighttime arrangements to take turns being up in the night with the baby. However, something happens when the new baby comes that throws a monkey wrench into the whole equality thing: the baby prefers the mother.

Blasphemous as it may seem to say so, there is a biological imperative that bumps up uncomfortably against our strivings for gender equality. Breastfeeding, essential to a baby's optimum health, necessitates exclusivity between baby and mother during the early months. This situation can contribute to a dad feeling left out and unsure of his own role and to a mom feeling overwhelmed.

In traditional societies, the new mother-baby dyad was protected by other women, grandmothers, and midwives. The protection was ritualized into a seclusion period of 30 to 40 days following the birth, during which the new mother and child rested, got to know each other, and established the milk supply. During this early time of adjustment, the mother was fed and taught by the experienced mothers, and the nursing couple was kept warm and protected from outside stimulation and infection. This seclusion period was essential to the survival of the new baby and mother.

Today, we seldom appreciate the need for an adjustment period, nor do we appreciate the special expertise of the mother. And yet a dormant instinctual, maternal intelligence is unlocked within a mother when she births her baby. We sometimes joke about "mother's intuition," but it is real. A lack of awareness of this situation, and of the importance of protecting the mother-child dyad, can further contribute to a new father's role confusion.

If a new father embraces an equal relationship with his wife, he may be discouraged when the baby prefers her. Because he knows that the baby doesn't want him, he may think he's done something wrong and be afraid to take care of the baby on his own. On the other hand, the new mother is often desperate for a break from the intensity of the new baby's needs, and legitimately needs help. Both mother and

father need to learn how to handle this new situation. For
example, the father will be more successful with the baby if he
takes the baby right after a good nursing. The mother must be
patient and encouraging as her husband learns how to hold
and change the baby and not undermine his confidence with
her own expertise.

While it is a biological imperative that makes the mother
and baby prefer one another during the early months, that
preference is also related to how much time they spend
together. Those dads who are around the baby a lot, engage
more with the baby, and are willing to be responsive to the
needs of mother and baby develop closer relationships with
their children sooner and perhaps more reliably.

After the first few months, when the breastfeeding relationship is fully established and becomes routine, the baby
reaches out for the father and then for the siblings and begins
to relate more to them. This delay in attachment can be hard
on dad, especially if he is proud of being an enlightened man.
Once he accepts the fact that the baby needs mom more in
the early months, his role becomes more obvious. His job is to
take care of the mother.

If the most important thing in our life is family, then family
has to come first. We must value ourselves not according to
cultural stereotypes but by how valuable we are to our family.
In the early years of parenting, this means putting the needs of
the mother first because she is putting the needs of the baby
first. This means self-sacrifice for mother and father, but sacrifice builds character and personal capacity. The baby's needs
are most urgent in the early years, when those needs require
constant physical contact. A healthy family will respond to
those needs unselfishly, not reluctantly or grudgingly.

In order for the family to respond unselfishly to the baby's
needs, the father and mother must redefine themselves. If
mothers take the lead and value themselves as mothers, then
their husbands will follow suit and learn to value themselves as
fathers and as helpmates. If a woman is ambivalent about her
own role as a mother and wonders why her husband doesn't
take a more active role, it may be because she is giving him
mixed messages. She may not be so sure of her own worth.

To avoid marital pitfalls, it is important to know our needs and to communicate openly and honestly. New parents often fail to talk about the expectations they have of one another. Unexpressed expectations and a lack of clear communication can make things rocky for a couple as they adjust to being new parents. There's a steep learning curve.

Conflict with our spouses in the early months and years is especially difficult because, as new mothers, we are dependent. Mothers are so accustomed to carrying on that they often don't recognize their needs until they are in emotional or physical trouble. And because they feel overwhelmed, they sometimes unfairly expect their partners to anticipate and meet their needs without being asked. Fathers, on the other hand, are eager to help but become discouraged when they are ineffective, when they don't know exactly what is needed, or when too much is expected of them. And they can feel oppressed by the wife's needs if their own needs go unrecognized.

Repeated conflicts over the same issues can hurt a marriage. If your first attempts to discuss such problems fail, set aside time by having dinner together or going for a walk. If talking fails, turn to self-help books, which can provide a shared language to communicate with. And while it should not be the first step, there is no failure in seeking help from a counselor, therapist, or clergy member. In fact, one trait of a healthy family is the ability to ask for help.

Happy couples disagree just as much as unhappy couples do. In stable marriages, however, positive behaviors outnumber negative behaviors by five to one. In unstable marriages, positive behaviors barely outnumber the negative. There are three types of stable marriages: the validating, the conflict-avoiding, and the volatile. In the validating marriage, the couple does not fight a lot—instead, they face issues, negotiate, and compromise. In order to negotiate and compromise, we have to learn how to listen. Everyone wants to be heard; but in good communication, it is also important to be able to show empathy and to be willing to deal with strong emotions and pain.

This last part is perhaps the hardest. So many strong emotions and so much suffering are involved in the transformation of becoming a parent—the reality of children washes away many ideals and stereotypes. Couples face disappointment, and they may face tragedy. The hurts of their own childhood may be triggered by parenthood. It can be tough. When the hard times are not acknowledged, it is even tougher.

We often don't admit our problems because we think they are our fault. Just as living in a bottle-feeding culture can make the normal adjustments of breastfeeding seem abnormal, so too can living in a materialistic society make the profound adjustment to parenthood seem mundane—especially for fathers, whose transition is rarely articulated.

The irony of the early months and years of parenting is that a shift occurs. While mothers bond with their children through nurturing, fathers bond through play. Once the attachment period is past and the child's survival is assured, it's all about dad. Dad is the gateway to the larger world.

Fathers must follow the lead of their wives in the early years, trusting their instinctual intelligence and mother's wisdom. It is real. And during those vulnerable early years, they must protect their wives and children. This is as it has always been in the animal kingdom.

Mothers must take responsibility for their own emotions, ask for help when they need it, and not blame their husbands when things go wrong. Sometimes things just fall apart.

None of this means that we abandon the quest for gender equality. True gender equality means relinquishing the presumption of tasks preassigned by gender. It means picking up the slack, doing whatever needs to be done—showing up, taking responsibility, not assuming special privilege. Gender equality requires that both mothers and fathers pay attention to how much milk is in the fridge, to when the toilet paper runs out, to changing the oil. For parents, it means putting family first. But this cannot be accomplished unless the needs of all family members are acknowledged and taken seriously. It cannot be accomplished without the courage to change.

From Mothering, *issue no. 129 (March–April 2005).*

what is
natural family living?

A FEW MONTHS AGO I GOT A CALL from a reporter who
wanted me to define *natural family living* for an article she
was writing for the *Seattle Times*. Just yesterday, a friend told
me that the article had turned up in the *Baltimore Sun*.
Until now I have resisted defining *natural family living* for
several reasons.

First, at its best, *natural family living* defies general definition because it is about discovering what is natural for each
individual. Second, I don't want parents to think they must
follow rules in order to be good at parenting. And third, natural family living is not a movement, a fad, or a custom. It is
about getting back to our roots as humans and rediscovering
the parenting skills that have sustained humans throughout
history and prehistory.

I got started with natural family living in the 1970s,
when my first babies were born. At that time, there was a
burgeoning natural-living movement that had been catalyzed
by young people who had gone "back to the land" during the
Vietnam War and rediscovered sustainable ways of living.

In the 1970s, for example, many of us grew our own
organic food, made our own herbal remedies, and searched
in second-hand stores for cotton clothing for our children.
These things were not yet popular enough to be widely
available.

When I became pregnant with my first child, I read all
the books I could get my hands on. I was a vegetarian who
didn't take over-the-counter drugs, and I wanted to continue

living with these values as I raised my babies. I needed living examples who would give me confidence in the natural way. I read the anthropological writings of Margaret Mead, in which she talked about common characteristics shared by tribal peoples. Babies in tribes are integrated easily into their societies. They are born at home, breastfed without restrictions, and held in arms. Children are not routinely separated from adults, and adults work with children in their arms or at their side.

I was inspired by tribal societies and by the idea of a life that would integrate my experiences as a woman with my experiences as a mother. I lived on a farm at the time, and that, too, gave me confidence in natural living. As a new mother, I understood that it was not having a baby but my social isolation that made motherhood oppressive. I wanted a bigger, more positive picture of motherhood than was popular at the time.

Of course, at that time, there was no such thing as natural family living. Many of us were just trying to figure out what it meant to do things in as natural a way as possible. And then as now, there were the purists, the extremists, and the "occasional natural livers."

My new knowledge of the natural world ran parallel with what I was learning about attachment parenting from my baby and from the La Leche League meetings I attended each month. Attachment parenting is very much a part of natural family living. It appreciates that the first three to five years of life are a critical period for developing trust, empathy, dependency, and optimism.

Natural family living views pregnancy and birth as normal bodily processes, not disease states. Therefore, interventions are avoided during pregnancy in favor of human interaction. A person interested in natural living, for example, might choose to have her midwife palpate her abdomen to determine the baby's size and age rather than opt for an intervention such as ultrasound.

Similarly, birth is seen as a normal event that does not require drugs or intervention. Birth is not perceived this way because women who embrace the natural way are more heroic or tolerant of pain. It is perceived this way simply because a drug-free mother and baby have distinct advantages. A mother avails herself of an ecstatic birth chemistry that unlocks a dormant, instinctual maternal intelligence; a baby begins life without having imprinted on drugs and awake enough to successfully breastfeed.

It is not surprising, then, that the ideas of natural family living meet at the intersection of instinct and science. Personal intuition is often supported by scientific evidence. Homebirth is a good example of this. Homebirth fosters the intimacy and privacy necessary for an optimum birth. Its safety is also supported by scientific evidence, evidence that consistently demonstrates that birth is safe in any setting.

The ideas of drug-free birth and homebirth are not dogmas but are good news. They become serious options only if one begins to trust in the natural order of things. Above all, natural family living is about this trust. It is not about making homebirth a dogma; it is about believing that it is safe. If we can believe that homebirth is safe, we will believe that birth in general is safe.

Breastfeeding is an obvious expression of natural family living. One can trust that human milk is the best food for a baby. One can trust, too, that a baby will wean in his or her own time. This is easier said than done in a culture where the vast majority of babies don't nurse past six months, but with subsequent babies it gets easier to rely on this trust. And again—like birth, natural family living is not about rules but about a way to see the world. It is about learning to trust in our own inherent wisdom and the wisdom of our babies.

This new—and very old—way of looking at the world is very much a process. As a new mom, I knew intellectually that touching my babies, for example, was a good thing, but I had to get used to it, and my babies taught me well. This does not mean I was a failure because I was in the process of trusting the natural way. Entering the world of natural family living means accepting that there is a time lag between our intellectual appreciation of an idea and our emotional assimilation of it.

In this regard, one basic and important idea is that of simply holding our babies. For humans, touch is a nutrient that is necessary for full human development. Babies' brains are stimulated by the kind of rhythmic movement and physical stimulation they were accustomed to in the womb. Some call this in-arms parenting; it's the way of the tribes that Margaret Mead and others have studied. It's important to hold and carry our babies in arms or in a sling, carrier, or backpack. We can trust in and respond to a baby's need to be held.

In addition to touch, children need to eat food that is in as natural a state as possible. It seems obvious to say that people interested in natural family living want to use foods with few additives and preservatives. Parents sometimes err on the side of caution where food and children are concerned. For example, when my children were young I had to back off my high standards on sweets; I began buying candy from vending machines and hiding it under their beds. We cannot isolate ourselves from society and are always mediating our values with those of others. That doesn't mean, however, that we abandon our values.

In natural family living, we want to trust in the body's innate capacity to heal itself and see illness as a necessary immune stimulant, not a bothersome nuisance. Accordingly, natural family living is cautious about medical interventions. Medical circumcision, for example, is questioned because the procedure's claimed benefits remain unsupported by scientific evidence. Vaccinations are also questioned so that parents can exercise informed consent. Both medical circumcision and vaccination are complex, personal matters for which there is no single, easy answer. Here in particular we fall back on trust in the individual, which is the foundation of natural family living. We trust both in the inherent integrity of the child's body and in the inherent authority of the parent to make decisions for the family.

The values of natural family living are the values that have sustained the human species for millennia. They are inspired by evidence of the historically successful practices of our species. Our ancestors, for example, lived in community; birth was a ritualized cultural act with customs that ensured safe outcomes. Women attended other women during birth. Today, science has confirmed that a woman is much less likely to have birth interventions if she births in the company of another woman.

Natural family living is about optimum survival, but it is not about making rules for proper behavior. That is the last thing we need. Parents don't need any more guilt or more inflated standards of perfection. This is the beauty of natural family living, which is about falling back into ourselves and trusting our own natures again. It is not about conforming to anything. Natural family living is about trust in the natural order of things, trust in the innate goodness and perfectibility of people, trust that each child is following his or her individual timetable for development. What this means practically is: Trust your body. Trust your baby. Trust yourself.

I know that it can be hard to trust ourselves as parents. We want to ascribe a dogma to others and invest our authority in them. It's easy for *Mothering*, or for me personally, to be seen as an authority. We publish articles with strong points of view and encourage parents to trust the legitimate needs of their babies. However, what we really hope for are authentic and original individuals, people who are thoughtful about their parenting choices and who look at all sides of an issue before making a decision. What is most natural, it seems to me, is the need to choose for ourselves. I have no disagreement with someone who has examined things carefully and made a decision different from my own. I just want to make sure she has all the information.

The ideas of natural family living have heart and meaning and are a sustainable way of caring for children. They are not a dogma. I want to know not that you have followed my way but that you know what your own way is. And I hope that you will realize that the current cultural values regarding birth and parenting are social constructs of our times. Only by reconsidering them will you have the whole picture, and only the whole picture is good enough for your child.

Here are *some* of the basic ideas of natural family living as I understand it:

- Pregnancy and birth are normal processes that do not require drugs or interventions.
- Breastmilk is the optimum food for humans.

- Cosleeping helps to facilitate successful breastfeeding and bonding.
- Mothers and babies need to be together, especially during the first three to five years of life.
- Human babies have a need to be touched and to be held in arms.
- It is important to cultivate a community of like-minded families for friendship, information, and support.
- Eat food that is in as natural a state as possible.
- The human body has the capacity to fight off illness without the use of drugs and interventions.
- Unstructured play is essential to the full development of the human imagination.
- Hitting and punishment are unnecessary when children's natural desire to cooperate is engaged to resolve conflicts.

This is not a complete list. Please let me know what natural family living means to you. Do you find these ideas helpful in your family life? Do they seem impossible to attain? What would you add to the list? Let me hear from you. Let's foster a broad sense of natural family even as we appreciate its long history and deep roots.

From Mothering, *issue no. 130 (May–June 2005).*

also from **mothering**

The Way Back Home
These essays on life and family by Peggy O'Mara, *Mothering* magazine publisher and editor, appeared in *Mothering* between 1983 and 1992. From diapering infants to coping with teens, Peggy transforms the everyday incidents of domestic life to create a warm, tender, thoughtful affirmation of traditional family values. 139 pages. $10.95

Having a Baby, Naturally
This evidence-based guide to safe, natural childbirth explains the full range of options—both conventional and alternative—that women need to understand in order to make smart, well-informed decisions about their pregnancies and births. By Peggy O'Mara. 341 pages. $17.95

Natural Family Living
Mothering magazine's guide to parenting! This comprehensive volume covers a vast range of timeless and contemporary issues in detail, with authority. It's all here, from the practical to the philosophical, from preconception to adolescence. This is *the* resource for parents who strive to make informed choices as they create a whole, healthy family environment. By Peggy O'Mara. 416 pages. $17.95

Cosleeping Reprint
The world's top scientists speak out! This reprint presents an exclusive compilation of research to back your instincts: cosleeping is proven to be safe, natural, and beneficial. Safety guidelines and solid information help you cosleep with confidence. Contributors include James McKenna, PhD, Peter Fleming, PhD, and many other esteemed experts. 40 pages. $6.50

To order,
visit *www.mothering.com* and click on or call 505.984.6294.